(1 Corinthians) Chapter 13 has become famous. Its extraordinary power is acknowledged not only by Christians but by a multitude of others. Foremost men acclaim it as marvelous, one of the literary wonders of the world, without perhaps at all appreciating the real drift of its teaching. What is it that it really says? The opening verse of 1 Cor. 8 has told us that it is love that edifies. This chapter expands that fact and shows us in the first place that the most shining gifts, if without love, are of no value; and in the second place that love is the force, even when gifts are present, that really accomplishes everything.[1] – F. B. Hole

The excellency of love above the power of speaking the languages of men and of angels ; above the power of understanding all mysteries ; above all faith, even of the highest kind ; and above the virtue of giving all one's goods to feed the poor, or one's body to be burned. All these endowments would be valueless without love.[2] – Albert Barnes

---

[1] Frank Binford Hole, *Hole's Old and New Testament Commentary*, Public Domain, stempublishing.com/authors/hole/.

[2] Albert Barnes, *Notes Explanatory and Practical*, Public Domain, Blackie and Son, Queen Street, Glasgow, South College Street, Edinburgh, and Warwick Square, London, 1845, Free Download, Archive.org., P. 167.

Love Never Fails

31 Thoughts on Love from 1 Corinthians 13

Dr. Bruce Hitchcock

Table of Contents

To God the Father, Jesus the Son, and the Holy Spirit: the only unconditional love I have ever or will ever experience.

See, then, what is the love of God, that he gave his Son from of old, and has never revoked the gift. He stands to his gift and continues still to give his dear Son to all who are willing to accept him. Out of the riches of his grace he has given, is giving, and will give the Lord Jesus Christ, and all the priceless gifts which are contained in him, to all needy sinners who will simply trust him.[3] – Charles Spurgeon

[3] Charles Spurgeon, *Immeasurable Love*, Public Domain, 1885, .romans45.org/spurgeon/sermons/1850.htm, P. 12.

PREFACE

The people we truly, deeply love and respect, live on inside of us. When we love another person, they have an impact on our lives.

Our parents, siblings, spouses, and our dearest friends outside of our family help mold and shape us. We acquire their nuances, habits, language, and many times their beliefs. These people that we love and who love us in return, become an unalterable part of who and what we are.

We laugh at the same humorous situations and jokes, and we cry at the same disasters of life. Other people recognize these similarities and they openly comment on them. We are all an emotional, reactional, and visual creation of our own individual choices and decisions. However, these life choices are also impacted by the others who we love and cherish.

We, as believers, say that we love God. However, do we allow Him to impact our lives? We have the Spirit of God living in us, but do we ever let it show? Do we love Him so much that we have openly expressed that love so that others will see it in our lives?

1. INTRODUCTION

Prayer

Our love is imperfect and, therefore, lacking. But you, O, Lord, are a compassionate and gracious God, slow to anger, abounding in love and faithfulness (Psalm 86:15). *...because Your love is better than life, my lips will glorify You* (Psalm 63:3). We are unworthy, but You, Oh, God are unmatched. We praise and honor You in the matchless name of Jesus, Amen!

Today's Scripture: John 15:13-14

Greater love has no one than this: to lay down one's life for one's friends. You are my friends if you do what I command.

Associated Scriptures

I found the one my heart loves (Song of Solomon 3:4).

I charge you: Do not arouse or awaken love until it so desires (Song of Solomon 8:4).

God is love. Whoever lives in love lives in God, and God in them. (1 John 4:16).

But the fruit of the Spirit is love, joy, peace, forbearance, kindness, goodness, faithfulness, gentleness and self-control. Against such things there is no law. (Galatians 5:22-23).

Correlative Quotes

...Christ's life was not a common one, it was not the life of an innocent person only, or the life of a mere man, but of a man in union with the Son of God; it was the Lord of glory and Prince of life, who was crucified, and slain; a life that was entirely at his own dispose; it had never been forfeited by sin, nor could it have been forced away from him by men or devils; it was laid down of and by himself, freely and voluntarily; and that "for", in the room, and instead of his people, as a ransom for them...[4] – John Gill

Paul now proceeded to elaborate on the fact that love surpasses the most important spiritual gifts. Some of the Corinthian Christians may not have possessed any of the gifts mentioned in the previous three lists in chapter 12, but all of them could practice love. Clearly all of them needed to practice love more fully. The fruit of the Spirit (Gal. 5:22-23) is a more obvious demonstration of the Spirit's presence in a life, and His control over a life, than the other gifts of the Spirit. Love is the most fundamental and prominent of these graces. The love in view is God's love, that He has placed in the believer by the indwelling Spirit, that should overflow to God and others. It is the love that only the indwelling Holy Spirit can produce in a believer and manifest through a believer. Fortunately, we do not have to produce it. We just need to cooperate with God by doing His will, with His help, and the Spirit will produce it.[5] – Thomas Constable

"I am His! I am His! I am different from other men! They may do what they will, for their judgment is yet to come, but I am different from them, for I am Christ's." I wish all Christians felt that the life they live is given to them that they may glorify Christ by it.[6] – Charles Spurgeon

---

[4] John Gill, John Gill's Exposition of the Entire Bible, 1810, Public Domain, Mathews & Leigh, London, P. 499.

[5] Thomas Constable, *Expository Notes of Dr. Thomas Constable*, Public Domain, planobiblechapel.org/constable-notes/, P. 232-233.

[6] Charles Spurgeon, A Song of My Beloved no. 3185 a sermon published on Thursday, February 17, 1910, Metropolitan Tabernacle, Newington. spurgeongems.org/vols55-57/chs3185.pdf

Author's Notes

INTRODUCTION

As I began this book on love, an old 50's song, *Love is a Many Splendored Thing*, kept running through my mind. It is a song that more than adequately describes the feelings and sensations of love as mankind experiences it. It is the deep love between a man and a woman that is expressed through other things wonderful and majestic in the world around us. "It's the April rose that only grows in the early spring" and "The golden crown that makes a man a king."[7]

Love is a Many Splendored Thing gives us an excellent picture of human, worldly love. Man's love and God's love may use the same word but they have two very different expressions. In spite of the many and profound differences, the deeply compassionate love that exists between a husband and a wife is a way that can express the passionate love that God has for His children. We see this fervent but gentle love in the Song of Solomon.

The Song of Solomon is an allegory. It is a song that is filled with symbolism. It is expressed as a man's and a woman's love for each other. Yet it is also a portrayal of the love between the believer and Christ. It is a picture of a deep love relationship painted in the truth of a beautiful courtship and marriage.

YOUNG LOVE

Young love is the purest and most innocent form of love. In the Song of Solomon, we are introduced to the bridegroom of all creation and the bride of faith, yet in the guise of a young groom and his bride exploring intimacy for the first time.

The Song of Solomon is also known as the "Song of Songs." There is no other song that can match it for its beauty. Solomon's ode to love is the picture of Christ's love for the church and His deep

---

[7] Andy Williams, *Love is a Many Splendored Thing*, metrolyrics.com/love-is-a-many-splendored-thing-lyrics-andy-williams.html

and graphic depiction of the personal way that Jesus loves us.

THE EROTIC VIEW

In my early years, I was not permitted to read the Song of Solomon. Unfortunately, in this masterful song, the world sees pornography, while the believer sees the depth of love that the Christian has for his Christ.

A BROADER VIEW

Many modern-day Bible scholars discount the deeply theological imagery of this song for a more casual interpretation of the sanctity of marriage. "but in recent decades 'there has been a notable trend toward the interpretation of the Song of Songs as human love poetry.'"[8] However, in doing so, they ignore the vast array of scriptures that identify God in the Old Testament and Jesus in the New as being the bride of Israel and ultimately of all those who believe in Him. (See Ezekiel 16:8-14, Jeremiah 31:32, Joel 1:8-13, Hosea 2:1-13, Matthew 22:2, 25:10, Ephesians 5:25-33, 2 Corinthians 11:2, and Revelation 22:9-10.) This is by no means a complete list of the places in scripture that explain this relationship.

GOD'S LOVE FOR MANKIND

God has always loved His creation with a deep and abiding love. He loves mankind distinctively. After all, God created us in His image. He loved Adam and Eve and cared for them both before and after their episode of defiance. Their act of disobedience opened the door to spiritual death and eternal punishment.

From the beginning chapters of Genesis to the end of Revelation there is one great principle, the justification of those who would believe in Jesus and make Him the Lord of their lives (Romans 10:9-10). *"For God so loved the world that He gave His one and only Son, that whoever believes in Him shall have eternal life"* (John 3:16).

Romans 5:8 explains, *"But God demonstrates His love for us*

---

8 Andrews University Seminary Studies, Spring 1989, Vol. 27, No. 1, 1-19. Copyright ©
1989 by Andrews University Press.

in this, while we were still sinners, Christ died for us." So great is God's love that He allowed the sacrifice of His Son, Jesus, so that we might be rescued from an eternity of retribution. Then, while we were in the throes of that unbelief and disobedience, He died for us.

SPIRITUAL APPLICATION

God has commanded us to love as He has loved us (Matthew 23:34-40). The love of God is an unconditional love (Ephesians 3:17-19). It is not important what we have done in our lives. "For all have sinned and come short of the glory of God" (Romans 3:23).

We are all guilty. Our guilt separates us from God. Unworthy man cannot have a love relationship with a perfect God. However, the love of God for His creation has provided us with a pathway to eternal life. That road to justification was paved with the blood of Christ.

But God, in His great love for us, has provided us with an escape for this life we now live. He has rescued us from a wondering, aimless life and granted us eternal life with Him in paradise.

As I write this poem, I ache all over. I fell a couple of days ago and my entire body was jostled. Now, every joint and muscle is complaining. I guess I am officially too old to run. At least if I do, I will just continue to show my stupidity.

Each day in these last years of my life brings a new lesson on aging. Lord, give me the knowledge that I need to get old gracefully and the wisdom to apply it. Amen!

Oh, How He Loves

Oh, how deeply Jesus loves,
A love that comes from up above.
A love we cannot understand,
That touches each and every strand.
A love that sweeps us to His grace
As we look upon His face.

A love we cannot comprehend.
As He takes us by our hand.

And leads us to that solemn place.
Where we will see Him face to face.
In Him we feel the warmth of spring,
Bringing hope to suffering.

It is a miracle we feel,
A love that none can ever steal.
Even when the day is dark,
His love provides the hidden spark,
That brings us life and keeps us sane,
Through the days of worldly pain.

And when we hear these words of love,
The sacrifice that cost His blood.
"It is finished" was the cry,
It brings a tear to every eye,
It knows the love that brought Him there,
To show us all how much He cares.

Oh, how He loves us, loves us still,
Oh, how He loves, our hearts to fill,
Oh, How He loves us, a love that's true.
Oh, How He loves us, me and you.

– Bruce

I am thankful for God's love for me. The price Jesus paid; I cannot repay. But the love available to me I will inwardly and outwardly express for the rest of my days.

Lessons within the Lesson

Describe unconditional love. Read these verses: 1 Peter 4:8, Colossians 3:14, and John 15:12

How does this love reveal itself in Christ's love for us? Read John 3:16, John 15:13, and Proverbs 10:12.

How does our salvation contribute to our love for others? Read especially Proverbs 17:17 and Romans 5:5.

Read Romans 12:9-10. Based on this verse and its command to obedience, how should we live in light of Christ's love?

2: LOVE IN MY WORDS

Prayer

I call to you, LORD, come quickly to me; hear me when I call to you. May my prayer be set before you like incense; may the lifting up of my hands be like the evening sacrifice. Set a guard over my mouth, LORD; keep watch over the door of my lips. Do not let my heart be drawn to what is evil so that I take part in wicked deeds along with those who are evildoers; do not let me eat their delicacies (Psalm 141:1-4). In Jesus name a pray, Amen!

Today's Scripture: 1 Corinthians 13:1

If I speak in the tongues of men or of angels, but do not have love, I am only a resounding gong or a clanging cymbal.

Associated Scriptures

And I, brethren, when I came to you, came not with excellency of speech or of wisdom, declaring unto you the testimony of God (1 Corinthians 2:1, KJV).

And my speech and my preaching was not with enticing words of man's wisdom, but in demonstration of the Spirit and of power (1 Corinthians 2:4, KJV).

For Christ did not send me to baptize, but to preach the gospel, not in cleverness of speech, so that the cross of Christ would not be made void (1 Corinthians 1:17, NASB).

The soothing tongue is a tree of life, but a perverse tongue crushes the spirit (Proverbs 15:4).

Correlative Quotes

Paul was not setting love in contrast to gifts in this

periscope. He was arguing for the necessity and supremacy of love if one is to behave as a true Christian.[9] – Thomas Constable

Whether Paul had ever seen Jesus in the flesh, he knows him in the spirit. One can substitute Jesus for love all through this panegyric (acclamation).[10] – A. T. Robertson

(These worldly attributes) ...being wholly outward things, underived from the love of GOD, void of all grace-union with CHRIST, and not an atom of the whole springing from the quickening influences of GOD the SPIRIT; all would profit me nothing![11] – Robert Hawker

Author's Notes

INTRODUCTION

Without love in our hearts, our words have no meaning. When we speak lovingly or even reverently out of an unregenerate, reprobate heart, our words become empty, hypocritical, and duplicitous. It is only when we have a heart that has been changed into the image of the love of Christ that can we speak the words of love.

Therefore, love begins with the metamorphic relationship that comes through salvation. However, a loving attitude and language must be learned as we grow in Christ. Philippians 1:9 says, *"And this I pray, that your love may abound still more and more in real knowledge and all discernment."* The action of spiritual growth is the key to a loving language. The Bible is replete with warnings and instruction on our walk and talk related to our tongue.

1. Avoiding Deceitful Speech: 1 Peter 3:10 explains, *"Whoever*

---

[9] Thomas Constable, Expository Notes of Dr. Thomas Constable, Ibid, P. 236.

[10] A. T. Robertson, *New Testament Word Pictures Volume 6*, this work is in the Public Domain. Copy Freely, hopefaithprayer.com/books/NewTestamentWork Pictures-Robertson.pdf, P. 1348.

[11] Robert Hawker, The Poor Man's New Testament Commentary, Volume 2, 1805, Public Domain, Printed by W. Nicholson, Warner Street, London, P. 151.

would love life and see good days must keep their tongue from evil and their lips from deceitful speech." Deceptive speech is not necessarily lying. However, blatant fabrication of the truth is included in the meaning of this verse. When our true feelings and thoughts are masked by our words, we are intentionally misleading those to whom we speak.

2. <u>A Language of Grace</u>: Colossians 4:6 tells us that we are to, *"Let your conversation be always full of grace, seasoned with salt, so that you may know how to answer everyone."*

3. <u>Building Up Others</u>: Ephesians 4:29 says, *"Do not let any unwholesome talk come out of your mouths, but only what is helpful for building others up according to their needs, that it may benefit those who listen."*

The English language contains only one word that is used to describe or identify the closest of all relationships, love. Love is a term of endearment. We use it to describe many things. "I love your new house." Or, I love my spouse to the moon and back." Then there is "I love a full moon on a warm summer evening." The word suggests that we love many things from our dog or cat to our children or grandchildren. We seem to recognize the different ways that we love things, but we are not always certain that others understand what we are attempting to communicate.

LOVE DEFINED IN THE GREEK

The Bibles that we use today are translations of Greek manuscripts. In fact, the word Bible is a transliteration of the Greek word Biblion or Biblos. Both words mean book.[12] In the Greek language, there are four words for love. Each word has its own unique meaning:

1. <u>Eros</u>: Sexual Love: This Greek word is not used in the New Testament.

---

[12] James Strong, Strong's Exhaustive Concordance, © 1890, Public Domain, Copy Freely, Christian Classic Reprints, P. 71.

2. Storge[13]: Family affection. This word is used in the New Testament for the warm affection that should exist between believers in Christ.

3. Philos[14]: Friendly Love. When joined with the word "adelphos" (brother), it means "Brotherly Love, as in the city of Philadelphia. It is used in the New Testament for our love for God and for others.

4. Agape[15]: Self-sacrificing Love. The word "agape" is the most forceful and fulfilling form of love. It uniquely describes God's love for us and our love for Him. It is unconditional love. Agape love is that deep and passionate love between God and His children that is initiated by faith in Him.

UNCONDITIONAL LOVE

Agape's love is God's love for us. In John 15:13, when Jesus says, *"Greater love has no one than this: to lay down one's life for one's friends"* the English word "love" is a translation of a form of the Greek word Agape. The ultimate sacrifice of God, a love without condition, represents the proof of the special love He has for mankind.

Agape love reaches out to another person with no strings attached. It is love that sacrifices itself on behalf of the one loved, with no thought of what might be received in return. This is the word that Paul uses in I Corinthians 13. It is love that starts with God, comes down to us, and then moves out from us to others.

LOVE AND THE TONGUE

James 3:6, *The tongue also is a fire, a world of evil among the parts of the body. It corrupts the whole body, sets the whole course of one's life on fire, and is itself set on fire by hell,"* helps us to understand the importance of the proper use of our words and the ways we use them in many and divergent circumstances.

---

[13] James Strong, Ibid, P. 386.

[14] James Strong, Ibid, #5384, P. 386.

[15] James Strong Ibid #26, P. 4.

What we say and how we say it can impact every relationship. This includes our communication with each other and our obedience to God. Proverbs 21:23 brings these thoughts about our language and its effect on others when it says, "*Those who guard their mouths and their tongues keep themselves from calamity.*"

SPEAKING LOVE

No matter what we say. No matter what language we speak it in. If our words are not spoken in love, it sounds like a clanging brass cymbal.

The Great Commandment (Matthew 22:36-40) tells us that we are first to love God. Secondly, we are to love others as we love ourselves. This might be confusing until we remember that we would do anything for ourselves. We think of what would be best for us in most decisions we make. We seldom will take responsibility or blame for anything we have done. We fight to see who is going to be first in line. Even in our language, we put ourselves first (Me and Tommy are going to the store).

Let us all remember Ephesians 4:15 when it says, "*Speaking the truth in love, we will grow to become in every respect the mature body of him who is the head, that is, Christ.*"

Spiritual Application

Recognizing others needs with comforting, supporting words clearly represents the first step in complying with the Great Commandment. Our words will wound or warm others.

The Great Commission wants us to place others before our selves. Jesus gives us the ultimate example. John, in John 15:13, explains this concept clearly when he writes, "*Greater love has no one than this: to lay down one's life for one's friends.*"

This action describes the extreme example of placing our friends and family ahead of self.

Now, there happened to be an occasion upon which the great God could display his immeasurable love. The world had sadly gone astray; the world had lost itself;

the world was tried and condemned; the world was given over to perish, because of its offenses; and there was need for help. The fall of Adam and the destruction of mankind made ample room and verge enough for love almighty. Amid the ruins of humanity there was space for showing how much Jehovah loved the sons of men... The far-reaching purpose of that love was both negative and positive; that, believing in Jesus, men might not perish, but have eternal life.[16] – Charles Spurgeon

Lessons within the Lesson

Read 1 John 3:18. Write this verse in your own words substituting your name for "Dear Children."

Compare 1 John 3:18 as it relates to 1 Corinthians 13:1. How do these two verses support each other?

Read James 2:15-16. Who is your brother and how should we respond in this situation?

Read Ephesians 4:29-32:

What is the purpose of our speech?

How do we control our tongue?

What are the implications of this verse as we apply it to our lives?

How would we appear to others when we decide to follow these directions from God?

How would we reflect the love of Christ with these verses in view?

---

[16] Charles Spurgeon, *Immeasurable Love*, p. 2.

3. LOVE IN OUR THOUGHTS

Prayer

Only You, Oh, Lord, can discern the thoughts of man. You have the power over all things and all the inhabitants of the earth. Continually remind us to think, act, and speak out of love and not anger this day. *"May these words of my mouth and this meditation of my heart be pleasing in your sight, LORD, my Rock and my Redeemer (Psalm 19:14).* In Christ's name, I pray, Amen!

Today's Scripture: 1 Corinthians 13:2

If I have the gift of prophecy and can fathom all mysteries and all knowledge, and if I have a faith that can move mountains, but do not have love, I am nothing.

Associated Scriptures

For truly, I say to you, until heaven and earth pass away, not an iota, not a dot, will pass from the Law until all is accomplished (Matthew 5:18, ESV).

Two or three prophets should speak, and the others should weigh carefully what is said. And if a revelation comes to someone who is sitting down, the first speaker should stop. For you can all prophesy in turn so that everyone may be instructed and encouraged. ...For God is not a God of disorder but of peace (1 Corinthians 14:29-33).

Did the word of God originate with you? Or are you the only people it has reached? If anybody thinks he is a prophet or spiritually gifted, let him acknowledge that what I am writing to you is the Lord's command. (1 Corinthians 14:36-38).

Correlative Quotes

But what I beg may be more particularly regarded by the reader is, the special limitation which this Epistle has to the Church at Corinth. Paul does not write to the Corinthians, as Corinthians; neither to the men of Corinth as of a province or place; but to the Church of GOD then in Corinth. It is the Church, not the world. And this is most essentially necessary to be kept in view all along, and through every part of this, and all the Epistles.[17] – Robert Hawker

Without "love" prophecy, knowledge, and faith, are not what they seem. ...and so, they fail to gain heavenly reward (Matthew 6:2).[18] – Jamieson, Fausset, Brown

At the conclusion of the preceding chapter the apostle promised to show the Corinthians a more excellent way than that in which they were now proceeding. They were so distracted with contentions, divided by parties, and envious of each other's gifts, that unity was nearly destroyed.[19] – Adam Clarke

AUTHOR'S NOTES

INTRODUCTION

The gift of prophecy, in the sense of 1 Corinthians 13:2, reflects the favor that God grants to pastors and teachers of the Word. God allows His chosen advocates to understand the deep mysteries of the scriptures that are the hidden thoughts of God. He no longer adds to His Word, the Bible, by speaking through prophets. The Bible is a completed book. Prophesying in this

---

[17] Robert Hawker, The Poor Man's New Testament Commentary, Volume 2, 1805, Ibid, P. 3-4.

[18] Jamieson, Robert, D. D.; Fausset, A. R.; Brown, David, Commentary Critical and Explanatory on the Whole Bible, Public Domain 1871, Public Domain, Copy Freely, P. 2511

[19] Adam Clarke, *The Adam Clarke Commentary Corinthians through Philemon*, Public Domain, © 1836, Thomas Tegg and Son, 73 Cheapside, London. godrules.net/library/clarke/clarkegen 1.htm, P. 133

sense means expounding on the word of God. Those who preach and teach open it words for themselves and others to understand truth that causes spiritual growth.

PROPHECY IN THE CHURCH TODAY

1. The Word, God's Complete Message to Mankind: Hebrews 4:12 says this about Scripture, *"For the word of God is alive and active. Sharper than any double-edged sword, it penetrates even to dividing soul and spirit, joints and marrow; it judges the thoughts and attitudes of the heart."*

   The complete story of God and His plan for the past, present, and future are already written in scripture. However, the interpretation of Scripture and its meaning for groups of people and individuals is a vital service. Prophetic office, as implemented today, involves identification, analysis, clarification, and explanation of what is already completed. Nothing can be added to or taken away from Scripture (Deuteronomy 4:2 and Revelation 22:18).

2. The Word, God's Tool For Salvation And Spiritual Growth: 2 Timothy 3:16-17 explains, *"All Scripture is God-breathed and is useful for teaching, rebuking, correcting and training in righteousness, so that the servant of God may be thoroughly equipped for every good work."* The Word of God is His tool for salvation, spiritual growth, and instruction in obedience continually convicting us of our unrighteousness.

3. The Word, A Living Document: Ephesians 3:16-19, *"I pray that out of his glorious riches he may strengthen you with power through his Spirit in your inner being, so that Christ may dwell in your hearts through faith. And I pray that you, being rooted and established in love, may have power, together with all the Lord's holy people, to grasp how wide and long and high and deep is the love of Christ, and to know this love that surpasses knowledge—that you may be filled to the measure of all the fullness of God."*

   Even though the Bible contains the complete Word of God, its depth of understanding continually changes. God's word, then, becomes an excellent tool for growth. Its teachings grow deeper as we move closer to God.

Spiritual Application

The source of all righteous love is God. The source of God's love is found in His Word, the Bible. When we believe in God and accept the gift of the Holy Spirit, a whole new world of spiritual depth is available to us.

Knowledge now becomes understanding (Proverbs 2:6).

Understanding unleashes wisdom (Proverbs 4:5-6).

Wisdom encourages application (1 Corinthians 4:16).

Application accelerates spiritual growth (2 Corinthians 9:10).

God's Love

How can it be that you would love,
A sinner such as me?
That you would pay the price of death,
For those who would believe.

Your love so unconditional,
I feel it in my soul.
The depths of your sincerity,
You have made me whole.

The gift of love, eternal life,
Given full and free,
To a sinful, meritless,
Unworthy one like me. – Bruce

Lessons within the Lesson

Can we understand the love of God? Read 1 John 4:7-12.

Explain how love changes as a result of salvation. Read Romans 13:10, Ephesians 4:2-3, and 1 John 4:11.

How will what we say determine how we love?

Read 2 Corinthians 2:14-15. Can unregenerate mankind understand the word of God?

4. LOVE IN MY WALK

Prayer

Lead us, Oh, Lord that we may walk in Your Spirit and under your direction. Open our hearts to those around us who are in need that we may serve You by sacrificing for them. Give us open hands that will enable us to reach out and touch the lives of others as Christ met the needs of those around Him. Help us to walk in love today and forever, Amen!

Today's Scripture: 1 Corinthians 13:3

If I give all I possess to the poor and give over my body to hardship that I may boast, but do not have love, I gain nothing.

Associated Scriptures

Carry each other's burdens, and in this way you will fulfill the law of Christ. 3 If anyone thinks he is something when he is nothing, he deceives himself. 4 Each one should test his own actions. Then he can take pride in himself, without comparing himself to somebody else, 5 for each one should carry his own load (Galatians 6:2-5).

And do not forget to do good and to share with others, for with such sacrifices God is pleased (Hebrews 13:16).

Give, and it will be given to you. A good measure, pressed down, shaken together and running over, will be poured into your lap. For with the measure you use, it will be measured to you" (Luke 6:38).

Give to the one who asks you, and do not turn away from the one who wants to borrow from you (Matthew 5:42).

...walk in love, just as Christ also loved you and gave Himself up for us, an offering and a sacrifice to God as a fragrant aroma (Ephesians 5:2).

Correlative Quotes

God grant that we, beloved brethren and sisters in Christ, may do our Lord's will so scrupulously, in great things and little things, and in all things alike, that those who see us in our daily life may be compelled to say, "Behold how these Christians love Jesus Christ their Lord and Savior!"[20] – Charles Spurgeon

It was a gratification to wealthy men who desired the praise of being benevolent, that many of the poor flocked daily to their houses to be fed; and against this desire of distinction the Savior directed some of his severest reproofs. See Matthew 6:1-4. To make the case as strong as possible, Paul says that if ALL that a man had were dealt out in this way, in small portions, so as to benefit as many as possible, and yet were not attended *with true love towards God and towards man*, it would be all false, hollow, hypocritical, and really of no value in regard to his own salvation. It would profit nothing.[21] – Albert Barnes

Because love brings the purest rapture. "Where is heaven?" asked a wealthy Christian of his minister. "I will tell you where it is, "was the quick reply : "if you will go to the store, and buy 10 lbs. worth of provisions and necessaries, and take them to that poor widow on the hillside, who has three of her children sick. She is poor, and a member of the Church. Take a nurse, and

---

[20] Charles Spurgeon, *Oh, How He Loves!* Public Domain, No. 3228 Delivered by C. H. Spurgeon, at The Metropolitan Tabernacle, Newington, On Lord's-Day Evening, July 7, 1872.

[21] Albert Barnes, *Notes Explanatory and Practical*, Public Domain, 1845, Free Download, Ibid., P. 2720.

someone to cook the food. When you get there, read the twenty-third Psalm, and kneel by her side and pray. Then you will find out where heaven is."[22] – F. B. Meyer

Author's Notes

INTRODUCTION

In 1 Corinthians 13:3, Paul says, in essence, if we give everything that we have to the poor and surrender ourselves completely to serve God and our motivation is not love, we gain nothing of which we desire. In addition, if we complete these actions hoping to receive honor, glory, and respect from mankind or from God, we are wasting our time, talent, and treasure.

GIVING CREDIT WHERE CREDIT IS DUE

All good things come as gifts from God. He is our provider. Through His grace and love, God supplies our needs. Paul says in Romans 11:35-36, *"Who has ever given to God, that God should repay him?" For from him and through him and to him are all things. To him be the glory forever! Amen."*

God's express purpose is to glorify Himself, not us. Psalms 115:1 (AMP) states, *"Not to us, O Lord, not to us but to Your name give glory, for Your mercy and loving-kindness and for the sake of Your truth and faithfulness!"*

> If you meet with a system of theology which magnifies man, flee from it as far as you can. If the minister, whom you usually hear, tries to make man out to be a very fine fellow, and says a great many things in his praise, you should let him have an empty place where you have been accustomed to sit. If it is man-praising, and man honoring, it is not of God.[23] – Charles Spurgeon

---

[22] Meyer, Fredrick Brotherton, Our Daily Homily, Public Domain, Grand Rapids, 1899, MI: Christian Fleming H. Revell Company, enduringword.com/downloads/our-daily-homily/, P. 146.

[23] Charles Spurgeon, "Non Nobis Domine," Public Domain, 1878, spurgeongems.org/vols46-48/chs2784.pdf, P. 4.

RESPONSIBLE STEWARDSHIP

There are sixty-six Books in the Bible containing 31,102 verses. In the NKJ version of the Bible, various forms of the word **"give"** appear approximately 3,300 times. This number represents about 10% of the total verses in the Bible. These three thousand verses represent more scriptures than the words, faith, hope, and love combined and tripled. We can see that giving is very important to God.

1 Timothy 6:17-19 (NKJV) commands *"...those who are rich in this present age not to be haughty, nor to trust in uncertain riches but in the living God, who gives us richly all things to enjoy. Let them do good, that they be rich in good works, ready to give, willing to share, storing up for themselves a good foundation for the time to come, that they may lay hold on eternal life.*

GOD PLANS OUR LIVES

God has a plan for our lives. God's plan or will for our lives is a perfect plan. We may think that we are in control of our destiny but Proverbs 16:9 (NKJV) says, *"man's heart plans his way, But the Lord directs his steps."*

God's plan or will for our lives includes all areas of our lives. Ecclesiastes 3:1-8 (NKJV) tells us that there is a time for every purpose under heaven: A time to be born, and a time to die; A time to weep, and a time to laugh; A time to mourn, and a time to dance; A time to gain, and a time to lose; A time to keep silence, and a time to speak; A time to love, and a time to hate. This also includes little things and big things in our lives. For example, our neighborhood and place of work are part of the plan of God.

God even gives us direction on who and who not to marry: 2 Corinthians 6:14 tells us, *"Do not be unequally yoked together with unbelievers. For what fellowship has righteousness with lawlessness?* God also provides direction with the number of children we have: Psalms 127:4-5 *"Like arrows in the hand of a warrior, so are the children of one's youth. Happy is the man who has his quiver full of them."*

God's Plan for our lives also includes how much and when

we should give. 1 Corinthians 16:2 suggests, *"On the first day of every week, each one of you should set aside a sum of money in keeping with your income, saving it up, so that when I come no collections will have to be made."*

God also gives us strong direction concerning our giving in 1 Timothy 6:17-19 (NKJV).

1. Don't be a Snob: (1 Timothy 6:17a) *"Command those who are rich in this present age not to be haughty..."* Don't be arrogant about the things that you have.

2. Don't Trust in the Unpredictable Wealth: (1 Timothy 6:17b) *"nor to trust in uncertain riches..."* Don't place your confidence in the world monetary system. When we place our hope in unreliable risk we gamble with the future.

3. Don't Ignore Sound and Responsible Advice: (1 Timothy 6:17c) *but* (trust) *in the living God..."* Pray and wait on God to supply certain leadership. 2 Corinthians 7:4 reads, *"Great is my confidence in you; great is my boasting on your behalf I am filled with comfort; I am overflowing with joy in all our affliction* ()*.*

4. Don't Forget the Gifts: (1 Timothy 6:17d) *"who gives us richly all things to enjoy."* God provides for our needs, not necessarily our wants. Every action of God pictures His grace. Philippians 4:19 explains, *"But my God will supply all our NEEDS according to the riches of His GRACE in Christ Jesus."*

5. Don't Neglect Our Part: (1 Timothy 6:18a) *"Let them do good, that they be rich in good works..."* Paul explains why in Ephesians 2:10, *"For we are His workmanship created in Christ Jesus to do good works which He has prepared for us beforehand for us to do."* God has created a good works disposition within us.

6. Don't Procrastinate: (1 Timothy 6:18b-19a) Paul continues to teach Timothy and us to be, *"ready to give, willing to share, storing up for themselves a good foundation for the time to come..."* When we practice good works, Jesus says in Matthew 6:19-21 that we are accumulating heavenly wealth, *"Do not lay up for yourselves treasures on earth, where moth and rust destroy and where thieves break in and steal; but lay up for*

yourselves treasures in heaven, where neither moth nor rust destroys and where thieves do not break in and steal. For where your treasure is, there your heart will be also."

7. <u>Don't Miss Out on God's Eternal Promises</u>: (1 Timothy 6:19b) *"that they may lay hold on eternal life."* NKJV. Our love is to be expressed to the world through our actions. We don't please God by loving what He has given us, but by using these gifts for His Glory. 1 John 2:15 commands that we *"Love not the world, neither the things that are in the world. If any man loves the world, the love of the Father is not in him."*

Spiritual Application

In verse 3, Paul isn't saying that believers shouldn't donate to the poor or that His children should neglect personal service to God. He explains instead that when they give, their responsibility is to assign all credit to God and not steal it for personal aggrandizement. The reflection of spiritual maturity diverts the attention and acclaim to gain personal attention or prominence. Christians are not to be the benefactors of the recognition.

Lessons within the Lesson

Why should we give God all the credit when we give to others or to Him? Read Colossians 3:22-24.

Why should believers give glory to God? Read Psalms 96:4-9.

Why are our "good works" important? Read and comment on Philippians 2:12-13.

How do we know what works God wants us to do? Read Ephesians 4:20-32.

5. LOVE IS PATIENT

Prayer

Lord, God, help us to be *"Be completely humble and gentle; be patient, bearing with one another in love. Make every effort to keep the unity of the spirit through the bond of peace"* (Ephesians 4:2-3).

Today's Scripture: 1 Corinthians 13:4a

Love is Patient (Love suffers long, NKJV).

...since the day we heard about you, we have not stopped praying for you and asking God to fill you with the knowledge of his will through all spiritual wisdom and understanding. And we pray this in order that you may live a life worthy of the Lord and may please him in every way: bearing fruit in every good work, growing in the knowledge of God, being strengthened with all power according to his glorious might so that you may have great endurance and patience, and joyfully giving thanks to the Father, who has qualified you to share in the inheritance of the saints in the kingdom of light. For he has rescued us from the dominion of darkness and brought us into the kingdom of the Son he loves, in whom we have redemption, the forgiveness of sins (Colossians 1:9-14).

Associated Scriptures

But if we hope for what we do not yet have, we wait for it patiently (Romans 8:25).

Wait for the Lord; be strong and take heart and wait for the Lord (Psalm 27:14).

Be completely humble and gentle; be patient, bearing with one another in love (Ephesians 4:2).

Be joyful in hope, patient in affliction, faithful in prayer (Romans 12:12).

Correlative Quotes

Now we are to contemplate more closely the features that characterize love. First comes a very positive feature. It suffers long (or, has long patience) and is kind. Could anything surpass the long patience and kindness of God's dealings with rebellious man? No. Well, God is love. And in the measure in which we manifest the divine nature, we shall manifest long patience and kindness towards men generally, as well as towards our brethren. ...This one positive feature is followed by negative features. Love is marked by the total absence of certain hideous deformities of character and behavior, which are perfectly natural to us as men in the flesh.[24] – F. B. Hole

The apostle next pointed out the qualities of "love" that make it so important—its character or nature. He described these in relationship to a person whose character love rules over. We see them most clearly in God and in Christ, but also in the life of anyone in whose heart God's love reigns.[25] – Thomas Constable

He now commends love from its effects or fruits, though at the same time these eulogiums (tributes or accolades) are not intended merely for its commendation, but to make the Corinthians understand what are its offices, and what is its nature. The object, however, mainly in view, is to show how necessary it is for preserving the unity of the Church. I have also no doubt that he designed indirectly to reprove the Corinthians, by setting before them a contrast, in which

---

[24] Frank Binford Hole, *Hole's Old and New Testament Commentary*, Public Domain, ibid.

[25] Thomas Constable, *Expository Notes of Dr. Thomas Constable*, Ibid, P. 237.

they might recognize, by way of contraries, their own vices.[26] – John Calvin

Author's Notes

INTRODUCTION

Most of us have heard the whimsical prayer, "Lord give me patience; and give it to me now!" Naturally, none of us would pray this prayer in earnest, but many times our actions speak louder than our words.

At some point in our lives, we have all been impatient. we may feel, for example, that we will never receive what we seek. Or, we just want our current circumstances to change to take off the pressure.

As a child, I thought Christmas, with its joy and of course, the presents, would never arrive. In another circumstance, I think of the birth of our first child. The anticipation of His arrival was overwhelming. We thought that he would never get here. My wife and I couldn't wait for life to begin a new normal.

THE DARK SIDE OF IMPATIENCE

Impatience has its consequences. The byproducts of waiting for resolution of the stress that causes it can be uncontrollable fear, frustration, fury and in some circumstances fractured relationships. Nothing good comes from impatience. The uneasiness caused by this reaction to pressure can be anything from a nuisance to a devastating occurrence.

PREPARING FOR PATIENCE

Patience is not an inborn characteristic. We continually see the results of impatience in children. Unfortunately, since it is more often placated than corrected when they are young, we see it commonly displayed in adulthood.

It is often thought that people must learn patience. However,

---

[26] John Calvin, *Commentaries on the Catholic Epistles*, Rights: Public Domain, URL: ccel.org/ccel/calvin/calcom 45.html., Publisher: Grand Rapids, MI. , P. 262.

attempting to develop this trait is counterproductive. It would take patience to learn patience. The world, which promotes and too often rewards impatience will not teach it to its followers. Even Psychologists seem to grow impatient while attempting to teach it to others.

CALM IN THE FACE OF THE STORM

Calm in the face of pressure takes wisdom. Since spiritual wisdom comes only from God, composure in the face of pressure is actually a gift from God. Therefore, it cannot be taught. Philippians 4:6 tells us, *"Do not be anxious about anything, but in every situation, by prayer and petition, with thanksgiving, present your requests to God."*

GODLY COMPOSURE, THE ANSWER TO STRESS

As in all issues of life, we must turn to God to resolve impatience. Proverbs 3:5-6 teaches us that all things are in God's hands and under His control. Colossians 1:9-14 gives us an outline for dealing with this life issue.

1. Let God Release Your Stress: (Vs. 9b), *"the knowledge of his will."* Proverbs 37:7 teaches us to wait on the Lord to act when it says, *"Be still before the LORD and wait patiently for him; do not fret when people succeed in their ways when they carry out their wicked schemes."* Knowing that God has a plan for our lives is always reassuring. His will on our behalf will overcome the greatest stress that the world can throw at us.

2. Live a Continually Renewed Life: (Vs. 10a), *"live a life worthy of the Lord."* By grace through faith we became transformed (Ephesians 2:8-9), a new creation in the spiritual likeness of Christ (2 Corinthians 5:17). We were rescued from sin and death simultaneously when we made Him the Lord of our lives (Romans 10:9-10). In addition, we are being renewed daily as evidence of our salvation. 2 Corinthians 4:16 confirms this point when it says, *"Therefore we do not lose heart. Though outwardly we are wasting away, yet inwardly we are being renewed day by day."* However, since the old sin nature continually tempts us, we must constantly renew the faith that brought us eternal life.

Colossians 1:22-23 substantiates this truth when Paul writes, *"But now he has reconciled you by Christ's physical body through death to present you holy in his sight, without blemish and free from accusation--if you continue in your faith, established and firm, and do not move from the hope held out in the gospel. This is the gospel that you heard and that has been proclaimed to every creature under heaven, and of which I, Paul, have become a servant."* Continual renewal of our faith is the evidence of internal spiritual change.

3. <u>Releasing Stress by Pleasing God</u>: (Vs. 10b) *"please him in every way."* Romans 12:1 encourages us by saying, *"Therefore I urge you, brethren, by the mercies of God, to present your bodies a living and holy sacrifice, acceptable to God, which is your spiritual service of worship."* We cannot please God if we are not being obedient to Him by following His plan for our lives.

> All that is done contrary to orders is disobedience, not service. And if anything is done without orders, it may be excessive activity, but it certainly is not service. Alas, my brothers and sisters, how many think they are serving God when they have never looked to the statute book; they have not turned to the commandments of the great King as we have them written in His word but have rendered to Him will-worship![27] – Charles Spurgeon

4. <u>Bearing Fruit that Remains</u>: (Vs. 10c) *"bearing fruit in every good work"* We are commanded to bear fruit through our good works. 1 Corinthians 15:16 tells us, *"You did not choose me, but I chose you and appointed you so that you might go and bear fruit-fruit that will last--and so that whatever you ask in my name the Father will give you."* New believers must be discipled (Matthew 29:18-20).

5. <u>Building Patience through Growing Spiritually</u>: (Vs. 10d) *"growing in the knowledge of God."* Ephesians 4:15 says, *"but speaking the truth in love, we are to grow up in all aspects into Him who is*

---

[27] Charles Spurgeon, Serving the Lord, Public Domain, 1869, spurgeongems.org/vols13-15/chs885.pdf., P. 3.

---

the head, even Christ." "The knowledge of God" provides us with the foundation for spiritual growth. Just as we must grow up physically and mentally from children to adults, we must "grow up" spiritually to become the mature Christians that God expects us to be.

6. Ensuring Patience by Trusting in the Spirit of God: (Vs 11) "being strengthened with all power according to his glorious might." Finally, we can only become patient through the power provided by the Holy Spirit. He lives in us to work God's will through us. 2Timothy 1:7 says, "For the Spirit God gave us does not make us timid, but gives us power, love, and self-discipline."

Spiritual Application

My good friend and retired pastor and missionary, Doyle Braden, says, "God never gives us patience until He first applies pressure and problems. When you are asking Him for patience you are saying to God, 'I am ready for the pressure and problems, Lord, bring it on.'"

God is faithful.

Lessons within the Lesson

How can we as an impatient people find the patience to deal in a Godly manner with all people? Read Ecclesiastes 7:9, Ephesians 4:2, and Galatians 6:9.

How does impatience impact our relationship with God? Read Philippians 4:6.

What does Romans 12:12 say about patience?

How does Proverbs 22:6 prepare us for having patience with grown children?

6. LOVE IS KIND

Prayer

Lord, God, we love and adore You. We bow down before You, oh giver of life now and everlasting. Thank You for Your great compassion. Without Your forgiveness, we have no hope of eternal life, Amen!

Today's Scripture 1 Corinthians 13:4b

Love is kind

Associated Scriptures

Do not let any unwholesome talk come out of your mouths, but only what is helpful for building others up according to their needs, that it may benefit those who listen. And do not grieve the Holy Spirit of God, with whom you were sealed for the day of redemption. Get rid of all bitterness, rage and anger, brawling and slander, along with every form of malice. Be kind and compassionate to one another, forgiving each other, just as in Christ God forgave you (Ephesians 4:29-32).

Don't have anything to do with foolish and stupid arguments, because you know they produce quarrels. And the Lord's servant must not quarrel; instead, he must be kind to everyone, able to teach, not resentful. Those who oppose him he must gently instruct, in the hope that God will grant them repentance leading them to a knowledge of the truth (2 Timothy 2:23-25).

A kind man benefits himself, but a cruel man brings trouble on himself (Proverbs 11:17).

Correlative Quotes

Patience and kindness, like love, are aspects of the fruit of the Spirit (Galatians 5:22). The first characteristic is love's passive response, and the second its active initiative. Patience and kindness characterize God, Christ, and truly Christian behavior.[28] – Thomas Constable

Here follows a description of love. Descriptions of positive characteristics and negations of evil qualities are now employed by the Apostle in what he would have us believe to be his impossible task of adequately describing true love.[29] – C. J. Ellicott

The word here used denotes to be good-natured, gentle, tender, affectionate. Love is benignant. (benevolent) It wishes well. It is not harsh, sour, morose, in-natured. Tindal renders it, "is courteous." The idea is, that under all provocations and ill-usage it is gentle and mild. Hatred prompts to harshness, severity, unkindness of expression, anger, and a desire of revenge. But love is the reverse of all these. A man who truly loves another will be kind to him, desirous of doing him good; will be gentle, not severe and harsh; will be courteous because he desires his happiness and would not pain his feelings. And as religion is love, and prompts to love, so it follows that it requires courtesy or true politeness and will secure it. See 1 Peter 3:8. [30] – Albert Barnes

Author's Notes

INTRODUCTION

Live in peace with each other. And we urge you, brothers, warn those who are idle, encourage the timid, help the weak, be patient with everyone. Make sure that nobody pays back wrong for wrong, but always try to be

---

[28] Thomas Constable, *Expository Notes of Dr. Thomas Constable*, Ibid, P. 237.

[29] Ellicott, C. J. (Charles John), A New Testament Commentary for English Readers, 1819-1905. Public Domain, Published by E. D. Dolton and Company, New York, 1897.

[30] Albert Barnes, *Notes Explanatory and Practical*, Public Domain, 1845, Free Download, Ibid.

kind to each other and to everyone else (1 Thessalonians 5:13-15).

Unity with others describes the purpose of kindness in the Christian life. Love provides the basis for unity. Kindness produces it. Conversely, disunity has its foundation in discord with others. Where there is animosity, hostility, and intolerance we always find disunity.

Kindness in Action

1. <u>Live in Peace with each other</u>: (1 Thessalonians 5:13b). Romans 5:1 says, *"now that we have been justified by His gift of faith, we now have peace with God."* Justification stems from God's forgiveness for our sin. When we forgive others for their transgressions and they forgive us for our indiscretions, we establish and maintain peace with each other.

   Forgiveness is a form of kindness. In fact, forgiveness is probably the greatest form of kindness. Forgiveness is a gift that we give to others who don't deserve it, just as God forgave us while we were being disobedient (Romans 5:8). Trust may be earned, but not forgiveness. If forgiveness could be earned, then there would have to be a standard for "sorriness" that would force forgiveness. There is no standard, just as there is no word sorriness.

2. <u>Warn those who are Idle</u>: (1 Thessalonians 5:14b). Ecclesiastes 10:18 explains that *"If a man is lazy, the rafters sag; if his hands are idle, the house leaks."*

   The man who pursues his pleasure when he should be doing his work will certainly find his business "decaying," his credit falling, his prospects of success "dropping through." So, also, the housewife, the student, the minister, the secretary, the statesman.[31] – Spence and Excel

   There is a difference between laziness and idleness.

---

[31] H. D. M. Spence and Joseph S. Exell, *The Pulpit Commentary*, Public Domain, Funk & Wagnalls Company New York And Toronto.

Laziness is not wanting to work or not keeping up with the quality or time limits based on the expectations of the job to be completed. Idleness is the complete refusal to work.

Both laziness and idleness have a lack of kindness in common. When a person is either lazy or idle, they are not being kind to their fellow workers or to those who have hired them. Idleness, or the complete lack of doing anything, speaks to the absence of all consideration for others. This may be why idleness head's Paul's list in 1 Thessalonians 5:14.

3. Encourage the Timid: (1 Thessalonians 5:14c). The ESV translates this section of the verse as, "*encourage the fainthearted.*" Timidity can also be defined as fear, anxiety, or even apprehension.

This timidity or fear is likely related to a future word or action. This act might be so grievous that it would separate them from their fellowship with other believers causing even greater angst.

Anxiety is a result of doubt. Doubt festers and becomes fear. Those who express apprehension require assurance to overcome their fright. Assurance would then meet the condition of encouragement.

Romans 8:38 is an example of assurance of eternal life. It explains that no created thing can separate us from the love of God that was established through the sacrifice of Jesus; nothing! If nothing can separate us from God's love, we have the assurance that our salvation is secure (1 John 5:13 and John 10:28).

4. Help the Weak: (1 Thessalonians 5:14d). If we would support the weak, those who cannot help themselves, we have this promise from God, "*Because the poor are plundered and the needy groan, I will now arise," says the LORD. "I will protect them from those who malign them*" (Psalm 12:5). God commands those who love Him to help the weak. "*we must help the weak and remember the words of the Lord Jesus, how he himself said, 'It is more blessed to give than to receive'*" (Acts 20:35).

5. Be Patient with Everyone: (1 Thessalonians 5:14e).

> ...patience towards all, for severity (effectiveness) must be tempered with some degree of lenity (tolerance), even in dealing with the unruly. This patience, however, is, properly speaking, contrasted with a feeling of irksomeness (aggravation), for nothing are we more prone to feel (worn) out when we set ourselves to cure the diseases of our brethren. The man who has once and again comforted a person who is faint-hearted, if he is called to do the same thing a third time, will feel I know not what vexation (irritation), no, even indignation (displeasure), that will not permit him to persevere in discharging his duty. So, if by admonishing or reproving, we do not immediately do the good that is to be desired, we lose all hope of future success. Paul had in view to bridle impatience of this nature, by recommending to us moderation towards all.[32] – John Calvin

6. Ignore those who Do You Wrong: (1 Thessalonians 5:15a). Romans 12:14 tell us to *"Bless those who persecute you; bless and do not curse."* Paul continues to refine this truth in verses 17 and 18 by saying *"Do not repay anyone evil for evil. Be careful to do what is right in the eyes of everyone. If it is possible, as far as it depends on you, live at peace with everyone."*

    These three verses, when combined with 1 Thessalonians 5:15a, lay the foundation for all kindness. Graciousness constitutes our attitude and actions toward others. We cannot say, "I am a kind person since I think kind thoughts." We may show consideration to other people. However, thinking amiable thoughts does not make us a kind person. It may help us to be compassionate but the thoughts are not kindness in themselves. Kindness is an action.

7. Be Kind to Each Other and Everyone Else: (1 Thessalonians 5:15b). Paul is saying don't just think kindly of others but bless

---

[32] John Calvin, *Commentaries on the Catholic Epistles*, Rights: Public Domain, Ibid, P. 184.

them. Blessing others represent the outward action of affection. When we act out compassionately toward those who persecute us, we not only confuse them, but we also display God's love through our kindheartedness to those who are watching to see our reaction. Paul concludes by encouraging us to treat all people with an attitude of love that represents peace.

Spiritual Application

It (kindness) is tender and compassionate in itself, and kind and obliging to others; it is mild, gentle, and benign; and, if called to suffer, inspires the sufferer with the most amiable sweetness, and the most tender affection. It is also submissive to all the dispensations of God; and creates trouble to no one.[33] – Adam Clarke

Kindness is related directly to faith. Faith is the reality of things that are hoped for and the evidence of things that we cannot see (Hebrews 11:1). When we have faith that God will bless our acts of kindness, we are more likely to perform graciously or amiably toward others. Kindness establishes us as being thoughtful to others.

A common interest, communal values, a willingness to reach an agreement, and kindness during the process, produce unity in relationships with others. Love seals them.

Lessons within the Lesson

Describe an unwarranted act of kindness you performed or that you saw carried out this week.

How do gracious thoughts lead to kind actions?

Why is kindness important to God? Read Ephesians 2:4-7.

What will be the result of kindness? Read Luke 6:35.

---

[33] Adam Clarke, The Adam Clarke Commentary Corinthians through Philemon, Public Domain, © 1836, Thomas Tegg and Son, 73 Cheapside, London. godrules.net/library/clarke/clarkegen 1.htm, P. 139.

7. LOVE DOES NOT ENVY

Prayer

Lord, God, help us not to envy anyone especially the wicked or wealthy. The world has blessed them because they have catered to its allurements. Keep us from those same temptations and protect us from the world and its sinful pleasures. Help us to be loving to all people. In Jesus name, Amen!

Today's Scripture: 1 Corinthians 13:4c

Love does not envy

Resentment kills a fool, and envy slays the simple (Job 5:20).

Associated Scriptures

Do not envy wicked men, do not desire their company; for their hearts plot violence, and their lips talk about making trouble. By wisdom a house is built, and through understanding it is established; through knowledge its rooms are filled with rare and beautiful treasures (Proverbs 24:1-4).

At one time we too were foolish, disobedient, deceived and enslaved by all kinds of passions and pleasures. We lived in malice and envy, being hated and hating one another. 4 But when the kindness and love of God our Savior appeared, 5 he saved us, not because of righteous things we had done, but because of his mercy. He saved us through the washing of rebirth and renewal by the Holy Spirit, 6 whom he poured out on us generously through Jesus Christ our Savior, 7 so that, having been justified by his grace... (Titus 3:3-7).

But if you harbor bitter envy and selfish ambition in your hearts, do not boast about it or deny the truth. 15 Such "wisdom" does not come down from heaven but is earthly, unspiritual, of the devil. 16 For where you have envy and selfish ambition, there you find disorder and every evil practice (James 3:14-16).

Correlative Quotes

When we see the wicked prosper, we are apt to envy them. When we hear the noise of their mirth and our own spirit is heavy, we half think that they have the best of it. This is foolish and sinful. If we knew them better, and especially if we remembered their end, we should pity them. The cure for envy lies in living under a constant sense of the divine presence, worshiping God and communing with Him all day long, however long the day may seem. True religion lifts the soul into a higher region, where the judgment becomes clearer and the desires are more elevated.[34] – Charles Spurgeon

(In Job 5:2) Eliphaz foresaw their ruin with an eye of faith. Those who looked only at present things blessed their habitation, and thought them happy, blessed it long, and wished themselves in their condition. But Eliphaz cursed it, suddenly cursed it, as soon as he saw them begin to take root, that is, he plainly foresaw and foretold their ruin; not that he prayed for it (I have not desired the woeful day), but he prognosticated it. He went into the sanctuary, and there understood their end and heard their doom read (Psalms 73:17,18), that the prosperity of fools will destroy them, Proverbs 1:32.[35] – Matthew Henry.

For - so far are you from profiting by your complaints. you only destroy yourself by justifying yourself and

---

[34] Charles Spurgeon, *Cure for Envy*, Public Domain, charlesspurgeon.nl/jaloezie-2/?lang=en, P. 1.

[35] Matthew Henry, Matthew Henry Commentary on the Whole Bible (Unabridged), Volume III (Job to Song of Solomon), Public Domain, 1706, bitimage.dyndns. org/., P. 65-66.

impatiently complaining against God. Foolish man ... silly one - imply at once the sin and folly of him who dreams he has merited nothing but good at Gods hands and is impatient at affliction being sent upon him. Wrath ... envy - fretful and passionate complaints, such as Eliphaz charged Job with (Job 4:5). So, Proverbs 14:30 - "Envy [is] the rottenness of the bones." For "envy," translate 'fretful passion kills the foolish.' Not, that the wrath of God kills the foolish, but His envy, etc.[36] – Jamieson, Fausset, and Brown

Author's Notes

INTRODUCTION

Envy, resentment, and hatred closely resemble each other. They represent the steps that we take as we walk down a path to overt spite.

Envy expresses itself as the unhappiness or discontentment that arises when others have something that we want but can't have.

Secondly, resentment originates as the reaction to the exasperation, or indignation from our inability to acquire what we deem unattainable.

Finally, anger is a reaction to the pain of hopelessness. It is generated by the helpless feeling that comes from the failure to gain what we can't have. Anger has many unhealthy outlets. None of them are positive nor do they please or glorify God.

Paul pleads with believers not to be caught up in the disobedient act of envy. He writes simply, *"Love does not envy."*

But in spiritual things it is not so, there is a... universal remedy provided in the word of God for all spiritual sicknesses to which man can be subject to; and that remedy is contained in the few words of my text (Isaiah

---

[36] Jamieson, Robert, D. D.; Fausset, A. R.; Brown, David, "*Commentary Critical and Explanatory on the Whole Bible*," Public Domain 1871, Ibid, P. 1088.

53:5), "*With His stripes we are healed.*" Not stripes laid upon our own backs, nor tortures inflicted upon our own minds, but the grief which Jesus has endured for those who trust in Him.[37] – Charles Spurgeon

Envy ushers us down an ugly road that leads to disappointment. Ultimately, displeasure with the unattainable incubates and hatches as hatred. If we don't find an answer for this "incarnation" we will slide into an attitude of hopelessness. Anger will eventually deafen our ears to the promises of rescue found in the Scripture. We will wander aimlessly in the control of the world system and not under the authority of God's Spirit.

THE CURE FOR ENVY

1. Seek God's Wisdom Instantly: Jeremiah 17:9-10, "*The heart is deceitful above all things and beyond cure. Who can understand it? I the LORD search the heart and examine the mind, to reward each person according to their conduct, according to what their deeds deserve.*"

   We must be continually aware of the temptations that the world is throwing at us. We are regularly encouraged to "keep up with the "Joneses." We buy something that we really want and very soon afterward the new model comes out and we feel like we need it. What makes it worse is we see someone we know who has the new model and we become envious.

   When we experience the first feelings of envy, we must act to placate them. We can appease these desires by seeking the wisdom of God. God's Word encourages us to be content with what we have. Philippians 4:12 says, "*I know what it is to be in need, and I know what it is to have plenty. I have learned the secret of being content in any and every situation, whether well fed or hungry, whether living in plenty or in want.*"

2. Pray for Direction Immediately: Psalm 139:23 (ESV), "*Search me, O God, and know my heart! Try me and know my thoughts!*

---

[37] Charles Spurgeon, *The Universal Remedy*, Public Domain, 1868, spurgeongems.org/vols13-15/chs834.pdf, P. 1.

And see if there be any grievous way in me and lead me in the way everlasting!" In this prayer in Psalms, believers are asking God to continually evaluate their spirituality. The psalmist is then praying that God will lead them now and forever. Allowing God to lead is the key to the joy that we seek through things; earthly things. However, true happiness is found only in God and obedience to Him.

3. Read the Scriptures Diligently: 2 Timothy 3:16-17 (ESV), *"All Scripture is breathed out by God and profitable for teaching, for reproof, for correction, and for training in righteousness, that the man of God may be complete, equipped for every good work."* Ecclesiastes 4:4 teaches and reproves us when Solomon writes, *"And I saw that all toil and all achievement spring from one person's envy of another. This too is meaningless, a chasing after the wind."* God knows all the questions, and He has all the answers. He has given us the answers to these questions in His Word, the Bible.

4. Trust in the Lord Completely: Psalm 62:8, *"Trust in him at all times, you people; pour out your hearts to him, for God is our refuge."* Lean on Jesus. Strength and power arise from the blood of the Lamb.

5. Be Thankful Eternally: Psalm 107:1, *"Give thanks to the LORD, for He is good; His love endures forever."* We cannot thank God often enough for what he has accomplished for us. We are His beloved creation. Created in His image. Created to do His will. When we are living in His will, we find the peace that He promised us when He said in John 14:27, *"Peace I leave with you; my peace I give you. I do not give to you as the world gives. Do not let your hearts be troubled and do not be afraid."*

  We have nothing to fear. God provides for all our needs. This is His promise to those who have made Him the Lord of their lives. Philippians 4:19 says, *"And my God will supply every need of yours according to his riches in glory in Christ Jesus."*

Spiritual Application

  Love and envy cannot coexist. Love overcomes envy. A

deep desire to own what others have exists inside us. Even small children at play will grab what others are using. The Bible and the world system both call this desire envy. As the envy grows it becomes resentment. We resent that others possess something or a relationship with someone that we can't have. Resentment builds into anger. All three of these reactions are sin (Proverbs 23:17 and Titus 3:3). Envy and its path to hatred destroy relationships. The relationship with God is in turmoil due to the person's sin nature once again battling against the Spirit (Romans 7:14-20). In addition, the relationships that we enjoy with those who we envy become broken as our hatred toward them builds.

To avoid envy we must turn to God. First, we must ask the Spirit of God for His wisdom. Along with wisdom and prayer, we should search God's word for understanding and strength. In addition, overcoming envy will require us to trust in God that He might fulfill His promise to keep us from temptation. Matthew 26:41 describes this promise when it reads, "*Watch and pray that you may not enter into temptation. The spirit indeed is willing, but the flesh is weak.*"

Lessons within the Lesson

What are the steps that will lead us to anger?

Explain how these steps (envy, resentment, to hatred) have impacted your life at some point in the past?

Explain how you have been able to overcome the feeling of envy with God's help?

How will you anticipate the feeling that initiates envy and how do you begin to correct it immediately?

8. LOVE DOES NOT BOAST

Prayer

Our Lord and our God help us to do our boasting in You and not in ourselves. We know in our hearts that all good things come from You. Help us to express our gratitude to You for all that we accomplish in a way that we are not bragging. Everything we enjoy in life comes from our position through Your gift of salvation. Praise Your Holy Name, Amen!

Today's Scripture: 1 Corinthians 13:4d

Love does not boast

In God we boast all day long and praise Your name forever (Psalms 44:8).

Associated Scriptures

I will bless the Lord at all times; His praise shall continually be in my mouth. My soul shall make its boast in the Lord ; the humble shall hear of it and be glad. Oh, magnify the Lord with me, And let us exalt His name together (Psalms 34:1-3).

Why do you boast of evil, you mighty man? Why do you boast all day long, you who are a disgrace in the eyes of God? Your tongue plots destruction; it is like a sharpened razor, you who practice deceit. You love evil rather than good, falsehood rather than speaking the truth (Psalms 52:1-3).

Do not boast about tomorrow, for you do not know what a day may bring forth. Let another praise you, and not your own mouth; someone else, and not your own lips (Proverbs 27:1-2).

Correlative Quotes

Those who are animated with a principle of true

brotherly love will in honor prefer one another, Romans 12:10. They will do nothing out of a spirit of contention or vain-glory, but in lowliness of mind will esteem others better than themselves, Philippians 2:3. True love will give us an esteem of our brethren, and raise our value for them; and this will limit our esteem of ourselves, and prevent the tumors of self-conceit and arrogance. These ill qualities can never grow out of tender affection for the brethren, nor a diffusive benevolence.[38] – Matthew Henry

The love of God, and of our neighbor for God's sake, is patient toward, all men. It suffers all the weakness, ignorance, errors, and infirmities of the children of God; all the malice and wickedness of the children of the world: and all this, not only for a time, but to the end. And in every step toward overcoming evil with good, it is kind, soft, mild, benign. It inspires the sufferer at once with the most amiable sweetness, and the most fervent and tender affection. Love acts not rashly - Does not hastily condemn anyone; never passes a severe sentence on a slight or sudden view of things. Nor does it ever act or behave in a violent, headstrong, or precipitate manner. Is not puffed up - Yea, humbles the soul to the dust.[39] – John Wesley

What I have rendered, ...does not act insolently is in the Greek. It is sometimes taken to mean, being fierce, or insolent, through presumption, this meaning seemed to be more suitable to the passage before us. Paul, therefore, ascribes to love moderation, and declares that it is a bridle to restrain men, that they may not break

---

[38] Matthew Henry, Matthew Henry Concise Commentary on the Whole Bible (Unabridged), Volume VI, Acts to Revelation, Public Domain, 1706, bitimage.dyndns. org/. P. 817.

[39] John Wesley, John Wesley's Notes of the Bible, Public Domain, Publication date 1755, jacobjuncker.files.wordpress.com/2010/03/wesley-explanatory-notes-on-the-bible.pdf#page=564&zoom=100,0,308, P. 319.

forth into ferocity, but may live together in a peaceable and orderly manner.[40] – John Calvin

Author's Notes

INTRODUCTION

> The fruit of the lips tends to vanity, poverty, to sorrow, to shame, to death. The fruit of the lips is just what the root of an unrenewed, unregenerate heart causes it to be.[41]
> – Charles Spurgeon

A lying, spiteful, and vicious tongue is the reflection of a reprobate heart. James 3:5-6 explains the evils of the tongue of the immoral when he writes, *"Likewise, the tongue is a small part of the body, but it makes great boasts. Consider what a great forest is set on fire by a small spark. The tongue also is a fire, a world of evil among the parts of the body. It corrupts the whole person, sets the whole course of his life on fire, and is itself set on fire by hell."*

BOASTING ABOUT OURSELVES

James 4:16 explains, *"As it is, you boast in your arrogance. All such boasting is evil."* Arrogance is having a lofty self-opinion. I believe it was Walt Whitman that once said, "If you done it, it ain't bragging." However, anything that we say about ourselves that is an attempt to show that we are better than another person or created thing is boasting.

Jeremiah 17:9 says this about the heart of man, *"The heart is deceitful above all things, and desperately wicked: who can know it?"* The nature of mankind celebrates unconformity to God and His Word. Instead of seeking God, unregenerate man clings to a world that will ultimately be judged and condemned for eternity. So, it is with his soul. The world system tempts mankind with its empty promises of health, wealth, and worldly goods. While all the time it has no intent to fulfill them. The world's reward includes unlimited disappointment and despair. The end is emptiness in life

---

[40] John Calvin, Commentary on 1 Corinthians, Public Domain, ibid, P. 263.

[41] Charles Spurgeon, *Rare Fruit*, spurgeongems.org/vols25-27/chs1558.pdf. P. 1.

accompanied by isolation in death and destruction in eternity. Not a pretty picture, but a truthful one.

The wealthy put on a good face. However, behind that facade is the torment of unrealized happiness, emptiness, and disillusionment. We are driven to find fulfillment in things when true satisfaction comes only from God.

BOASTING IN THE LORD

Instead of boasting about what we have accomplished in our own power or lying about things we haven't done, we should brag about what God has done. In addition, we should boast about those things He has finished that have little or nothing to do with us.

1. Jesus has Redeemed us: Ephesians 1:7, "*In him we have redemption through his blood, the forgiveness of sins, in accordance with the riches of God's grace.*" We have been bought with a price. That price is the blood of Christ. A blood offering had to be made for the sin of mankind. Only God himself could provide the perfect sacrifice that was required. God in the form of Jesus paid that debt.

2. He Provided Our Salvation as a Free Gift: Ephesians 2:8-9 (ESV), "*For it is by grace you have been saved, through faith — and this not from yourselves, it is the gift of God not by works, so that no one can boast.*" God has prevented our boasting by making the payment for our sin himself and offering that payment to us free of charge. John 1:12 says, "*But to all who did receive him, who believed in his name, he gave the right to become children of God, who were born, not of blood nor of the will of the flesh nor of the will of man, but of God.*"

3. He has given Us His Peace: Romans 5:1 (ESV), "*Therefore, since we have been justified by faith, we have peace with God through our Lord Jesus Christ.*" We who now believe, were, at one time, at war with God. We found ourselves hopelessly lost. Entangled in the world system. We grabbed and fought for everything we could accomplish in our own power. We struggled with others to make a name for ourselves. Then, we boasted, "Look at me. Look what I have done." We sought recognition

from a world that didn't care or at most pretended that it did. We stole the honor and glory from God. He who created us and loved us so much that He died for us was ignored and discredited.

Then, we were drawn by the Spirit of Him who saved us and we confessed Him as the Lord of our lives. Now, we recognize His power and presence. We see His plan for our lives. As a result, we give Him all honor and glory.

4. He is Preparing a Place for Us in Eternity: 2 Corinthians 5:1-5, "*Now we know that if the earthly tent we live in is destroyed, we have a building from God, an eternal house in heaven, not built by human hands. Meanwhile, we groan, longing to be clothed with our heavenly dwelling because when we are clothed, we will not be found naked. For while we are in this tent, we groan and are burdened, because we do not wish to be unclothed but to be clothed with our heavenly dwelling so that what is mortal may be swallowed up by life. Now it is God who has made us for this very purpose and has given us the Spirit as a deposit, guaranteeing what is to come.*" As a result of our salvation, we no longer bask in our own empty boasting but render to God His full due. In addition, we have discovered a newfound relationship with God and His relationship with us, the reposeful and soothing essence of His presence.

As believers, we seek His continual presence. We long for the time when we will serve Him, no longer in fleshly, sinful bodies but in glorified bodies: "Houses" prepared specially for us" (John 14:2) There is no room for boasting in that thought, only basking.

Spiritual Application

The boastful nature of mankind, fueled by an uncaring, callous, and resentful world, reflected in our arrogant thoughts and words is a direct affront to God and His nature of love.

At one point in my life, I used the humorous phrase, "The characteristic I am most proud of is my humility." In addition to poor English, this was bad humor. Pride is the root of all sin. It was pride that forced Satan and his angels out of their lofty position in Heaven. Pride is the very core of sin and unrighteousness. It is the heart of Satan's power and the goal of the world. It lies at the center of all temptation.

Prides greatest expression is boasting. It says, "I am in control and look what I have done." Pride robs God of His position of majesty.

The Power to overcome boasting can only come from God's Spirit. Our outward vain expressiveness is the attitude and language of self- aggrandizement or self-glorification. God wants the glory. Complete humility is the answer. We must pray for the Spirit of God to give us meekness. Aviod arrogant speech and practice humility.

Proverbs 27:2 teaches, "*Let another praise you, and not your own mouth; a stranger, and not your own lips.*" Proverbs 11:2 explains, "*When pride comes, then comes disgrace, but with humility comes wisdom.*"

Lessons within the Lesson

According to Romans 12:2, what is the taboo assigned to the world system and how do we resist its temptations?

Is Satan responsible for our sin? Read James 1:13-15.

Who controls the world system? Read Ephesians 2:1-3.

Is temptation the same as sin?

Do the devil and his angels have ultimate power?

9. LOVE IS NOT PROUD

Prayer

We know that in your Psalms, Lord, You say, "In his pride, the wicked man does not seek him; in all his thoughts there is no room for God." We desire to focus on You, Lord, but instead, we continually think only of ourselves. Help us, Oh, God, to live according to Your plan and Your purpose for us. In Your resolute name, we pray, Amen!

Today's Scripture: 1 Corinthians 13:4f

Love is not Proud

For who makes you different from anyone else? What do you have that you did not receive? And if you did receive it, why do you boast as though you did not (1 Corinthians 4:7)?

Associated Scriptures

If, in fact, Abraham was justified by works, he had something to boast about — but not before God. What does the Scripture say? "Abraham believed God, and it was credited to him as righteousness" (Romans 4:2-3).

For it is by grace you have been saved, through faith — and this not from yourselves, it is the gift of God—not by works, so that no one can boast. For we are God's workmanship, created in Christ Jesus to do good works, which God prepared in advance for us to do (Ephesians 2:8-10).

Who is wise and understanding among you? Let him show it by his good life, by deeds done in the humility that comes from wisdom. But if you harbor bitter envy and selfish ambition in your hearts, do not boast about it or deny the truth. ...instead, you ought to say, "If it is the

Lord's will, we will live and do this or that." As it is, you boast and brag. All such boasting is evil (James 4:13-16).

Correlative Quotes

Charity is careful not to pass the bounds of decency; ...it behaves not unseemly; it does nothing indecorous, nothing that in the common account of men is base or vile. It does nothing out of place or time; but behaves towards all men as becomes their rank and ours, with reverence and respect to superiors, with kindness and condescension to inferiors, with courtesy and good-will towards all men. It is not for breaking order, confounding ranks bringing all men on a level; but for keeping up the distinction God has made between men, and acting decently in its own station, and minding its own business, without taking upon it to mend, or censure, or despise, the conduct of others. Charity will do nothing that misbecomes it.[42] – Matthew Henry

(Love) Is not puffed up with pride, which is closely related to party zeal, as in those at Corinth who cried "I am of Paul, and I of Apollos," etc. Does not seek to win praise or applause.[43] – H. D. M. Spence and Joseph S. Excell

(Love) is not puffed up swelled with pride, and elated with a vain conceit of himself, of his parts (physical appearance) and abilities, of his learning (level of education), eloquence (speaking ability), wisdom, and knowledge, as the false teachers in this church were; knowledge without grace, unsanctified knowledge (other than Godly), mere notional speculative knowledge (their words and thoughts not the thoughts of God), puffed up;

[42] Matthew Henry, Matthew Henry Commentary on the Whole Bible (Unabridged), Volume VI, (Acts to Revelation), Ibid, P. 817-818.

[43] H. D. M. Spence and Joseph S. Exell, *The Pulpit Commentary*, Public Domain, ibid,

but charity, or the grace of love, does not; that edifies (instructs and enlightens) and perseveres persons from being puffed up with themselves, or one against another.[44] – John Gill

Author's Notes

INTRODUCTION

The prelude of destruction is pride, and of honor, humility. There is nothing into which the heart of man so easily falls as pride, and yet there is no vice which is more frequently, more emphatically, and more eloquently condemned in Scripture.[45] – Charles Spurgeon

When we *"rightly divide the word of truth"* (1 Corinthians 4:7), we see three common elements of pride. First and foremost, prideful people attempt to show that they are different from and better than other people. They laud themselves through personal flattery. They also honor themselves instead of God.

Secondly, those who are prideful take full credit for all they have achieved. Everything we have and every good work that we accomplish comes from God. Psalm 138:8 tells us that God is in control when we allow Him to administer our lives, *"The LORD will fulfill his purpose for me; your steadfast love, O LORD, endures forever. Do not forsake the work of your hands."*

Finally, a person's pride forces them to lie or exaggerate the personal claims of their accomplishments. Unfortunately, there are Christians who fall into all three of these categories.

1. <u>Pride Puts us on the Pedestal</u> (1 Corinthians 4:7a): *"For who makes you different from anyone else?"*

One under the influence of spiritual pride is more apt to instruct others than to inquire for himself and so

---

[44] John Gill, *Commentary of the Whole Bible*, Public Domain, 1816, Ibid., P. 302

[45] Charles Spurgeon, *Pride and Humility, 1856, Public Domain,* spurgeon.org/resource-library/sermons/pride-and-humility#flipbook/, P. 1.

naturally puts on the airs of control. The eminently humble Christian thinks he needs help from everybody, whereas he that is spiritually proud thinks everybody needs his help. Christian humility, under a sense of other's misery, entreats and beseeches, but spiritual pride tries to command and warn with authority.[46] – Jonathan Edwards

The implied answer to the first question in verse seven of 1 Corinthians four is no one. Prideful people attempt to separate themselves from those to whom they feel superior. One method involves judging others. The only group of people who have the right to judge others are those to whom God has assigned that task. This group would include public officials, police at all levels of law enforcement, fireman, clergy, and others who God chooses to rule over us.

1 Peter 2:13-17 explains, "*Therefore, submit yourselves to every ordinance of man for the Lord's sake, whether to the king as supreme, or to governors, as to those who are sent by him for the punishment of evildoers and for the praise of those who do good. For this is the will of God, that by doing good you may put to silence the ignorance of foolish men, as free, yet not using liberty as a cloak for vice, but as bondservants of God. ...Fear God. Honor the king.*" God has assigned these officials to protect us from the evil that is in the world. They will be responsible for how they adjudicate their responsibilities.

2. Pride Forces us to Take Credit: (1 Corinthians 4:7b), "*What do you have that you did not receive?*"

Another effect of spiritual pride is a certain self-confident boldness before God and men. Some, in their great rejoicing before God, have not paid sufficient regard to that rule in Psalm 2:11 — Worship the Lord with

---

[46] Jonathan Edwards, Undetected Spiritual Pride – One Cause of Failure in Times of Revival, grace-abounding.com/Articles/Sin/Pride_Edwards.htm, P. 1.

reverence, and rejoice with trembling.[47] – Jonathan Edwards

When we begin to understand that God owns everything (Deuteronomy 10:14) and calls all the shots in our lives (Proverbs 16:9), we see that He deserves all the credit (Isaiah 42:12). When we choose to take credit, we are robbing God of that honor. However, many times it is difficult to reflect the glory to God and not sound hypocritical.

False humility in itself can be an indicator of dishonesty and reflect pride. Saying something to avoid giving ourselves or God direct credit is sometimes helpful. An example would be, "Our strength to do these things comes from God." Or in another example, "I just try to remember that wisdom is a gift from God." Deflecting the power or understanding to God without making ourselves out to be something special is sometimes a difficult task.

3. <u>Pride Forces Us to Lie and/or Exaggerate</u>: (1 Corinthians 4:7c), *"And if you did receive it, why do you boast as though you did not?"*

Psalms 31:14 tells us, *"Let their lying lips be silenced, for with pride and contempt they speak arrogantly against the righteous."* This verse speaks primarily to unbelievers who would mock God and His teaching. However, Christians are not immune to pride. Pride causes those who seek honor and glory for themselves to exaggerate and often lie to make themselves look superior to others.

In the 1970s on a television program titled Can You Top This, pitted three comedians against the home audience as to who could tell the funniest story. The panel of three would be given a topic and they would have to fabricate a funny story. The audience would then vote to determine who on the panel or the entry from a home viewer had contributed the funniest story.

Prideful people always want to have the best story since

---

[47] Jonathan Edwards, Ibid.

their goal or aim is built on control. They may choose a true story, but they embellish the truth to make it better than another person's tale. There is nothing wrong with a great story. However, when we exaggerate the details, we are lying.

4. Pride Hinders the Work of Believers: **Proverbs 29:23,** *"A man's pride brings him low, but a man of lowly spirit gains honor."*

> The first and worst cause of errors that abound in our day and age is spiritual pride. This is the main door by which the devil comes into the hearts of those who are zealous for the advancement of Christ. It is the chief inlet of smoke from the bottomless pit to darken the mind and mislead the judgement.[48] – Jonathan Edwards

When dealing with others, a person's attitude is critical. If the believer exudes pride and arrogance rather than humility and reserve, the person to whom we are communicating, witnessing, or discipling will be inattentive. Too often our words speak so loudly that the message gets lost. We must remember to have the same attitude of love and compassion to others as Jesus showed to the crowds and to His disciples.

In John 21:15-17 (NKJV), Jesus and the Apostle Peter have an interesting exchange. Jesus begin the conversation by saying, *"Simon, son of Jonah,* do you love Me more than these?" He (Peter) said to Him, "Yes, Lord; You know that I love You." He (Jesus) said to him, "Feed My lambs." He (Jesus) said to him (Peter) again a second time, "Simon, son of Jonah,* do you love Me?" He said to Him, "Yes, Lord; You know that I love You." He (Jesus) said to him (Peter), "Tend My sheep." He said to him the third time, "Simon, son of Jonah,* do you love Me?" Peter was grieved because He said to him the third time, "Do you love Me? And he said to Him, "Lord, You know all things; You know that I love You." Jesus said to him, "Feed My sheep."*

When asking the first two questions to Peter, Jesus uses Greek form of the word Agape which means a deep, selfless,

---

48 Jonathan Edwards, Ibid.

unconditional love. Peter answers with a figure of the Greek word phileo meaning the love of a close friend or brother. Jesus says Peter do you love me with self-effacing, sacrificial, unqualified love. Peter says I love you like a brother."

Peter shows confusion with his answers. Jesus has not yet been crucified. So, Peter does not understand the sacrifice that Jesus will make on His and mankind's behalf. He has not yet seen the risen Christ. He has not yet received the gift of the Holy Spirit and therefore cannot understand the sacrificial love that Jesus describes in His use of the word agape.

Jesus, on this third question, makes an interesting change. He no longer uses the word agape but instead changes to Peter's word phileo. In this great act of humility, Jesus comes down to Peter's understanding of love to clear satisfy Peter's angst.

"This is my commandment, that you love one another as I have loved you" (John 15:12).

5. Pride Cripples Spiritual Growth:

It is by spiritual pride that the mind defends and justifies itself in other errors and defends itself against light by which it might be corrected and reclaimed. The spiritually proud man thinks he is full of light already and feels that he does not need instruction, so he is ready to ignore the offer of it.[49] – Jonathan Edwards

Spiritual growth is the anchor that protects us from the storms of life that would hamper our quest for God. It is the river of the water of life that flows from the throne of God (Revelation 22:1). It is the relentless waves of the ocean that bring oxygen and life to the sea. Spiritual growth is the lifeblood of our relationship with God (1 John 1:7). Our growth in knowledge, understanding, and wisdom lead to spiritual application. Pride, on the other hand, ties our spirits in knots and handcuff us by keeping the truth at bay.

---

[49] Jonathan Edwards, Ibid.

6. Pride Alters Our Relationship with God (1 John 1:7) *"When pride comes, then comes shame; but with the humble is wisdom."*

When we are living according to pride we cannot be in close fellowship with God (1 John 1:7). The Holy Spirit then convicts us of that disobedience and we must choose to continue in our pride or walk with the Spirit. Galatians 5:17 tells us, *"For the flesh desires what is contrary to the Spirit, and the Spirit what is contrary to the flesh. They are in conflict with each other so that you are not to do whatever you want."*

Spiritual Application

Proverbs 16:18 (ESV) says *"Pride goes before destruction, and a haughty spirit before a fall."* These simple but profound words explain the many and daunting perils of pride for both unbelievers and believers alike. God has given us many choices in life. We can choose to live the exemplary life that God has planned for us or we can choose to live a life filled with pride.

Pride will cause us heartache, pain, and separation from others rather than the honor and glory we seek. Living a life of humility and servanthood by giving God the honor and glory, will give us the respect we seek from others. The inner joy provided by the fruits of the Spirit gives us comfort, hope, faith, and allows us to express love to others. Pride is the joy blocker.

Joy in the Christian life is best received by continually giving it away.

Lessons within the Lesson

How does pride force us into lies? See Psalm 31:18

Why is focusing on ourselves being disobedient to God? Read Romans 8:7-9.

What impact does pride have on our spiritual growth? Read Proverbs 16:5, 16:18-19, and Romans 12:3-8.

How do we become aware of our pride and avoid it?

10. LOVE HONORS OTHERS

Prayer

Oh, Lord, my Lord, how we wish to serve you in our walk and talk. Help us to watch our words that we might not offend others with what do or say. We are your sheep and as such need direction in our lives. Keep us close by your side that we might always be prepared to speak your words and not ours, carry out your approved actions instead of those that we feel are appropriate. We wish to serve your purposes and not those of mankind. Show us Your amazing grace every moment of every day. In your remarkable name and through your inescapable love, we pray, Amen!

Today's Scripture: 1 Corinthians 13:5a

Love does not dishonor others

Be devoted to one another in brotherly love. Honor one another above yourselves. Never be lacking in zeal, but keep your spiritual fervor, serving the Lord. Be joyful in hope, patient in affliction, faithful in prayer. Share with God's people who are in need. Practice hospitality. Bless those who persecute you; bless and do not curse. Rejoice with those who rejoice; mourn with those who mourn. Live in harmony with one another. Do not be proud but be willing to associate with people of low position. Do not be conceited. Do not repay anyone evil for evil (Romans 12:10-17)

Associated Scriptures

Sacrifice thank offerings to God, fulfill your vows to the Most High, and call upon me in the day of trouble; I will deliver you, and you will honor me (Psalms 50:14-15).

The fear of the Lord teaches a man wisdom, and

humility comes before honor (Proverbs 15:33).

To those who by persistence in doing good seek glory, honor and immortality, he will give eternal life. But for those who are self-seeking and who reject the truth and follow evil, there will be wrath and anger (Romans 2:7-8).

Correlative Quotes

...in showing mutual respect and honor, they were to strive to excel; not to see which could obtain most honor, but which could confer most, or manifest most respect. ...How different this is from the spirit of the world; the spirit which seeks not to confer honor, but to obtain it; which aims not to diffuse (extend) respect, but to attract all others to give honor to us.[50] – Albert Barnes

We must not be ambitious of honor and preferment, nor look upon worldly pomp and dignity with any inordinate value or desire but rather with a holy contempt. ...Instead of contending for superiority, let us be proactive by giving others the pre-eminence. This is explained, Philippians 2:3, Let each esteem others better than themselves.[51] – Matthew Henry

"In brotherly love be affectionate one to another; in [giving, or showing] honor, outdoing each other." The word rendered "prefer" means rather "to go before," "take the lead," that is, "show an example." How opposite is this to the reigning morality of the heathen world![52] – Jamieson, Fausset, and Brown

---

[50] Albert Barnes, *Notes Explanatory and Practical*, Public Domain, Free Download, ibid, P. 2310.

[51] Matthew Henry, Matthew Henry Concise Commentary on the Whole Bible (Unabridged), Volume VI (Acts to Revelation), Public Domain, 1706, Ibid P.657-659.

[52] Jamieson, Robert, D. D.; Fausset, A. R.; Brown, David, Commentary Critical and Explanatory on the Whole Bible, Public Domain 1871m Copy Freely, ibid, P.2425.

Author's Notes

1. <u>Give Honor to all People</u>: (Romans 12:10) *Be devoted to one another in brotherly love. Honor one another above yourselves.*

In the 1960s there was a song sung by Aretha Franklin and written by Otis Redding entitled RESPECT. In the first stanza of the song, a lady reflects on the fact that she isn't getting the respect she deserves from the man she loves.

> "What you want
> Baby, I got it
> What you need
> Do you know I got it?
> All I'm askin'
> Is for a little respect..."

As believers and followers of Christ, we need to honor others. We must respect them for who they are not what we want them to be. We are required to value other's positive contributions whether or not we would agree with the execution. Finally, we are charged with admiring others for what they have accomplished in life.

We all desire the respect of others. However, we will only receive the admiration we seek when we learn to rightly honor others.

2. <u>Be Excited About Serving Others and God</u>: (Romans 12:11) *Never be lacking in zeal, but keep your spiritual fervor, serving the Lord.*

Excitement or enthusiasm furnishes the rush we feel as signature events happen in our lives. These occurrences can stem from experiences that are seen, written, or heard. The greatest surge of excitement occurs with the blessing that we receive from serving others.

Since outward acts of kindness to others is a commandment from God, His Spirit excites and delights us with feelings of His grandeur or majesty. God is glorified by these actions. He continually encourages us to do good works in His name. *In the same way, faith by itself, if it is not accompanied by*

---

action, is dead. We must serve God continually, with eagerness, earnestness, and enthusiasm. He has saved us to do His work here on earth (Ephesians 2:10).

3. Be Permanently Passionate, *Be Patient in Pain, Pray Persistently*: (Romans 12:12) *Be joyful in hope, patient in affliction, faithful in prayer.*

Paul explains that we must be continually filled with the joy of the Lord. James 1:2 (ESV) encourages us to, "*Count it all joy, my brothers, when you meet trials of various kinds, for you know that the testing of your faith produces steadfastness.*"

Suffering from physical pain can be debilitating. However, pain and suffering can express themselves in many ways other than physical. Emotional illness can be devastating. Stress can impact a person's behavior causing them to strike out at others.

Whether the disorder is physical or emotional we must not give up hope. Hope finds solace in prayer and patience. Healing comes only from trusting in God and the endurance to wait on His will to be completed in our lives (Isaiah 40:31).

4. Help the Needy: (Romans 12:13) *Share with God's people who are in need. Practice hospitality.*

James 2:14-17 says this about help for those in need, "*What good is it, my brothers, if a man claims to have faith but has no deeds? Can such faith save him? Suppose a brother or sister is without clothes and daily food. If one of you says to him, "Go, I wish you well; keep warm and well fed," but does nothing about his physical needs, what good is it?*

5. Bless those who Curse Us: (Romans 12:14) *Bless those who persecute you; bless and do not curse.*

We have all heard the phrase, "I don't get mad, I get even." This thought, though often used as humor, is not the reaction that God expects from His Children. Instead of getting even with someone who hurts us, God commands that we bless them. To bless another person means to wish them good will not ill will. When we issue someone a blessing who has hurt us, we extend to them the same grace that God extended to us. We must follow the example of Paul when he offered grace and peace to the church at Corinth in 2 Corinthians 1:2.

6. <u>Express Joy and Yet Mourn when Appropriate</u>: (Romans 12:15) *Rejoice with those who rejoice; mourn with those who mourn.*

Be joyful for others whether we are pleased with our circumstances or not. The joy expressed to others will always reflect positively our own inner joy. Joy is a treasure that all believers can share. Sharing it not only affects others, it also infects us.

At the grave of Lazarus, our Savior evinced (declared) this in a most tender and affecting (touching) manner. The design of this direction is to produce mutual kindness and affection and to divide our sorrows by the sympathies of friends. Nothing is so well fitted to do this as the sympathy of those we love.[53] – Albert Barnes

7. <u>Be Consistently Cooperative</u>: (Romans 12:16) *Live in harmony with one another. Do not be proud but be willing to associate with people of low position. Do not be conceited.*

There exists no inequality with God. We are all equal in God's eyes. Deuteronomy 10:17 testifies to the truth when Moses writes *"For the Lord, your God is God of gods and Lord of lords, the great God, mighty and awesome, who shows no partiality and accepts no bribes.*

He created us all, each one unique. However, no one is greater than anyone else. Matthew 23:11 explains that "The greatest among you will be your servant." He died for each of us when we were all equally guilty of disobedience (Romans 5:8).

8. <u>Be At Peace with all People</u>: (Romans 12:17) *Do not repay anyone evil for evil.*

And what a beautiful figure is added by the Apostle of

---

[53] Albert Barnes, *Notes Explanatory and Practical*, Public Domain, 1845, Free Download, Ibid., P. 2317.

heaping coals of fire on the adversary's head. Not to hurt, neither to expose him to the anger of the LORD; but to meltdown his angry passions, and to win him over to the cause of GOD and CHRIST, Oh! the blessedness of that grace of the LORD, which, when in lively exercise in the heart, can, and will, enable a poor sinner thus to feel for another poor sinner; and in the contemplation of the blessed JESUS, to recompence good for evil, and to overcome evil with good![54] – Robert Hawker

Spiritual Application

Giving honor to others requires humility on our part. When we honor other Christians for their spirit led words or actions, we also honor God. Glorifying God opens the spiritual door to the abundant life we are promised in Jesus (John 10:10). Ephesians 2:10 says this about our good works, *"For we are God's handiwork, created in Christ Jesus to do good works, which God prepared in advance for us to do."*

Lessons within the Lesson

Why is salvation by grace through faith alone and devoid of anything we have done on our own? Read Ephesians 2:8-9.

What is the purpose of good works? Read Ephesians 2:10.

Explain God's view of the equality of mankind. Read James 2:1-9.

In light of the title of this chapter, explain James 2:14-17.

---

[54] Robert Hawker, The Poor Man's New Testament Commentary, Volume 2, 1805, Public Domain, Ibid, P. 166.

11. LOVE IS NOT SELF-SEEKING

Prayer

We know, Oh Lord, that Your thoughts are not our thoughts and that Your ways are not our ways. As the heavens are higher than the earth, so are Your ways are higher than ours and your thoughts exceed ours. We know that Your words, Oh God of Heaven, will not return to You empty, but will accomplish what you desire and achieve the purpose for which they were sent (Isaiah 55:8-9, 11). Help us our Lord, to understand Your words this day that we might live a life that is pleasing to You. Our Father in Heaven, Holy and Exalted is Your name, a name above all names. We honor You, O, God, and You alone, Amen!

Today's Scripture: 1 Corinthians 13:5b

Love is not self-seeking

It does not seek its own way (ESV).

Associated Scriptures

But I tell you, love your enemies and pray for those who persecute you (Matthew 5:44).

If you love those who love you, what reward will you get? Are not even the tax collectors doing that (Matthew 5:46)?

God is love. Whoever lives in love lives in God, and God in him. In this way, love is made complete among us so that we will have confidence on the day of judgment, because in this world we are like him (1 John 4:16-17).

Correlative Quotes

...is it a violence (note: disservice) to this scripture, or will it be thought imaginary, if I were to say, might not

Paul have his LORD in view all along, as he drew the portrait?[55] – Robert Hawker

(Note: Love) seeks not her own things: even those which are "lawful", as the Arabic version renders it; but seeks the things of God, and what will make most for his honor and glory; and the things of Christ, and what relate to the spread of his Gospel, and the enlargement of his kingdom; and also the things of other men, the temporal and spiritual welfare of the saints: such look not only on their own things, and are concerned for them, but also upon the things of others, which they likewise care for: is not easily provoked: to wrath, but gives place to it: such an one is provoked at sin, at immorality and idolatry, as Paul's spirit was stirred up or provoked, when he saw the superstition of the city of Athens.[56] – John Gill

(Note: Love) Seeks not her own ease, pleasure, honor, or temporal advantage. No, sometimes the lover of mankind seeks not, in some sense, even his own spiritual advantage; does not think of himself, so long as a zeal (Note: passion) for the glory of God and the souls of men swallows him up.[57] – John Wesley

Author's Notes

INTRODUCTION

Love does not seek its own reward. True love does not demand or even expect anything in return. It is not self-absorbed or self-centered. Love is the outward expression of a deeper feeling.

---

[55] Robert Hawker, The Poor Man's New Testament Commentary, Volume 2, 1805, Public Domain, Ibid, P. 153.

[56] John Gill, John Gill's Exposition of the Entire Bible, 1810, Public Domain, Ibid, P. 302-303.

[57] John Wesley, *John Wesley's Notes of the Bible*, Public Domain, Publication date 1755, ibid, P. 320.

Love is centered in its sacrificial nature. It sees that good in all God's creation. Loving is the reward in itself.

SELFLESSNESS

1. <u>Selfless Love is not Egotistical</u>: Philippians 2:3, *"Do nothing out of selfish ambition or vain conceit, but in humility consider others better than yourselves."*

Love is never preoccupied with self. The loving Christian always puts the needs of others ahead of self. We live in a culture that says, "Me first, look at me." Spiritual love is other-directed. It is not self-love.

Jesus never thought of His own needs. He was only concerned about others. Luke 9:58 reads, *"Jesus replied, 'Foxes have dens and birds have nests, but the Son of Man has no place to lay his head.'"*

At the last supper, John 13, Jesus predicts His own death. It is pictured through the breaking of the bread and the drinking of the cup. Afterward, Judas departs to betray Jesus. It is at this point that Jesus (John 13:34) states, *"A new command I give you: Love one another. As I have loved you, so you must love one another."* God's love is all-inclusive. It has no limits; no boundaries.

2. <u>Selfless Love is not Selfish</u>:

Christians do not love expecting something in return. Believers do not expect personal gain or special favors in return for the action of selflessness. Love has no strings attached. It always gives with no regard for the sacrifice.

Self-denial might be considered an antonym to selfishness. It speaks to a meek spirit. In the Sermon on the Mount, Jesus gives us a list of eight characteristics of selfless believers. Reading the third beatitude we see in Mathew 5:5 *"Blessed are the meek, for they will inherit the earth."* A Spirit-controlled life is a God-pleasing life. Jesus was meek. Philippians 2:5-7, *"In your relationships with one another, have the same mindset as Christ Jesus: Who, being in very nature*

God, did not consider equality with God something to be used to his own advantage; rather, he made himself nothing by taking the very nature of a servant, being made in human likeness."

The reward for selflessness is a spiritual treasure. Deep happiness has its birth in pleasing God through service to others. Spiritual joy is different from worldly happiness. Joy is eternal while happiness is temporal.

3. <u>Selfless Love has no Conditions</u>: Spiritual love treats everyone equally.

The greatest example of unconditional love would have to be Christ's suffering and death on the cross. This was a true act of selflessness. Jesus was the perfect man. Hebrews 5:9 explains, *"And having been made perfect, He became, to all those who obey Him, the source of eternal salvation."*

Jesus lived a sinless life. 2 Corinthians 5:21 says, *"He made Him who knew no sin to be sin on our behalf so that we might become the righteousness of God in Him."*

Spiritual Application

We are to love as Jesus loved. When we look at the selfless nature of perfect love, we see Jesus. He was never egotistical. Instead, Jesus put others needs ahead of His own. He was unselfish. This giving nature extended to all those who He fed as well as those who were healed. He resurrected, and to His physical sacrifice on the cross. Christ's love is unconditional. It applies to everyone equally. He is not willing that anyone should perish. He wants everyone to have eternal life (1 Peter 3:9). Jesus had a servant's heart. That is the definition of selflessness.

Lessons within the Lesson

Explain the difference between selflessness and egotism.

How does selflessness bring us joy?

How is spiritual joy different from worldly happiness?

Explain the nature of unconditional love. How is this love unconditional?

12. LOVE IS NOT EASILY ANGERED

Prayer

Our Lord and God, in your Proverbs You write, "Fools give full vent to their rage, but the wise bring calm in the end. Direct us to avoid the foolishness of unwarranted rage with its awkward and embarrassing outcomes. Lead us instead to a spirit of calm at all times and in all circumstances. Fill us with your wisdom, Amen!

Today's Scripture: 1 Corinthians 13:5c

Love is not easily angered

Associated Scriptures

Be angry, and yet do not sin; *do not let the sun go down on your anger , and do not give the devil an opportunity* (Ephesians 4:26 -27).

*This you know, my beloved brethren but everyone must be quick to hear, slow to speak and **slow to anger;** for the anger of man does not achieve the righteousness of God* (James 1:19- 20).

A fool always loses his temper, but a wise man holds it back (Proverbs 29:11).

Correlative Quotes

(Comments on Mark 3:5) Jesus was angry that men should be silent when honesty and candor demanded speech of them. You must not think you are going to escape by saying, "I am not a professor." There can be no third party in this case. In the eternal world, there is no provision made for neutrals. Those who are not with Jesus are against him, and they that gather not with him are scattering abroad. You are either wheat or tares, and there is nothing between the two. Sirs, you grieve him though you do not openly oppose him! Some of you are especially guilty, for you ought to be amongst the foremost of his friends. Shame on you to treat the Lord so ill![58]. Charles Spurgeon

Here it means evidently to rouse to anger; to excite to indignation or wrath. Tyndale renders it, "is not provoked to anger." Our translation does not exactly convey the sense. The word "easily" is not expressed in the original. The translators have inserted it to convey the idea that he who is under the influence of love, though he may be provoked that is, injured, or though there might be incitements to anger, yet that he would not be roused, or readily give way to it.[59] – Albert Barnes

Such (a person) is provoked at sin, at immorality and idolatry, as Paul's spirit was stirred up or provoked, when he saw the superstition of the city of Athens; and is easily provoked to love and good works, which are entirely agreeable to the nature of charity[60] – John Gill

Author's Notes

INTRODUCTION

"The Lord passed before him and proclaimed, 'The Lord, the Lord, a God merciful and gracious , slow to anger , and abounding in steadfast love and faithfulness, keeping steadfast love for thousands, forgiving iniquity and transgression and sin, but who will by no means clear the guilty, visiting the iniquity of the fathers on the children and the children's children, to the third and the fourth

---

[58] Charles Spurgeon, Jesus Angry with Hard Hearts , romans45.org/ spurgeon/ sermons/ 1893.htm, P.7.

[59] Albert Barnes, *Notes Explanatory and Practical*, Public Domain, , 1845, Free Download, Ibid., P. 2727.

[60] John Gill, *Commentary of the Whole Bible,* Public Domain, 1816, Ibid, P. 303.

generation." It takes a great deal of disobedience to make God mad. Psalm 103:8 supports this statement when it says, "*The Lord is merciful and gracious, slow to anger and abounding in steadfast love.*"

ANGER AND THE BELIEVER

1. <u>Don't Anger Easily</u>: Proverbs 17:27, "*A man of knowledge uses words with restraint, and a man of understanding is even-tempered.*"

James 1:19-20, "*...everyone must be quick to hear, slow to speak and slow to anger; for the anger of man does not achieve the righteousness of God.*" This verse explains God's plan for interaction. When we are engaged in conversation and reacting to others, respond with purpose and caution.

"*Be quick to hear*": God says, dominate the listening. Pay attention to the details. Listen closely to the person's words, the tone, and body language. Don't interrupt. Allow the person to exhaust their point before responding.

Be slow to speak. Think before acting. Prepare a proper response. Pause long enough to allow forethought. Proverbs 10:19 reads, "*When words are many, sin is not absent, but he who holds his tongue is wise.*" In any possible confrontational situation, believers must be well prepared before speaking. Proverbs 12:18 stresses this point by saying, "*Reckless words pierce like a sword, but the tongue of the wise brings healing.*

2. <u>God's Anger</u>: Proverbs 6:16-19, "*There are six things the LORD hates, seven that are detestable to him: haughty eyes, a lying tongue, hands that shed innocent blood, a heart that devises wicked schemes, feet that are quick to rush into evil, a false witness who pours out lies and a person who stirs up conflict in the community.*"

God acts out His anger in the form of wrath. However, His wrath can be averted through prayers of repentance. He is a God of justice, but He is also a God of love. Psalms 6:1-4 states, "*O Lord, do not rebuke me in your anger or discipline me in your wrath. Be merciful to me, Lord, for I am faint; O Lord, heal me, for my bones are in agony. My soul is in anguish. How long, O Lord, how long? Turn, O Lord, and deliver me; save me because of your unfailing love."*

3. <u>Righteous Indignation</u>: Psalms 7:11 (TLB), *"God is a judge who is perfectly fair, and He is angry with the wicked every day."*

Is anger always a sin? The simple answer is no. If showing anger was a sin, God would have sinned throughout history. Ephesians 4:26a states, *"Be angry, and yet do not sin..."* How is this possible? Anger is only a sin when displayed or acted on. In addition, there are times when anger is appropriate.

Hearing the statistics on the number of abortions in the world and here in America should make us angry. Acting out appropriately by counseling women who have an unwanted or unaffordable pregnancy, providing help for them and the baby after the birth, and voting to pass laws that restrict abortion would be an appropriate reaction to inevitable anger.

Spiritual Application

Love is slow to anger. When reflecting on God we as believers are subject to God's anger and His eventual wrath due to our disobedience. However, we are protected by His great love. The love displayed by Jesus on the cross (1 John 2:1-2).

Lessons within the Lesson

How can we be angry and yet not sin?

How does God demonstrate His anger?

What things anger God? Read Proverbs 6:16-19. List each act of disobedience and explain why each one provokes His anger.

What placates God's anger? Read 1 John 1:7-10.

13. LOVE KEEPS NO RECORD OF WRONGS

Prayer

Jesus, our Lord, and Savior, we all are guilty before you. Therefore, convict us to *"Bear with each other and forgive one another."* Free us to overlook any grievance that we have against each other. Help us to forgive as You have forgiven us, Lord, (Colossians 3:13).

Today's Scripture: 1 Corinthians 13:5d

Love keeps no record of wrongs.

For as high as the heavens are above the earth, so great is his love for those who fear him; as far as the east is from the west, so far has he removed our transgressions from us (Psalm 103:11-12).

Associated Scriptures

Be kind to one another, tenderhearted, forgiving one another, as God in Christ forgave you (Ephesians 4:32, ESV).

And whenever you stand praying, forgive, if you have anything against anyone, so that your Father also who is in heaven may forgive you your trespasses (Mark 11:24, ESV).

But if you do not forgive others their trespasses, neither will your Father forgive your trespasses (Matthew 6:15, ESV).

Correlative Quotes

Dear friends, "there is forgiveness." nature could never tell you this great truth of God. You may walk the cornfields at this moment and see the bounty of God in the waving grain, but you cannot read forgiveness there.

You may climb the hills and see the beauty of the landscape. You may look upon silver streams that make glad the fields, but you cannot read forgiveness there. You can see the goodness of God to man, but not the mercy of God to sinners! But if you come to this Book, you can read it here.[61] – Charles Spurgeon

The meaning is, …that one possessed of this grace of love does not think of the evil that is done him by another; he forgives, as God has forgiven him, so as to forget the injury done him, and remembers it no more…[62] – John Gill

But is it not a frequent case that persons, who have received any kind of injury, and have forborne to avenge themselves, but perhaps have left it to God; when evil falls upon the sinner do console themselves with what appears to them an evidence that God has avenged their quarrels; and do at least secretly rejoice that the man is suffering for his misdeeds? Is not this, in some sort, rejoicing in iniquity?[63] – Adam Clarke

Author's Notes

1. God Forgives: 1 John 1:9, "*If we confess our sins, he is faithful and just and will forgive us our sins and purify us from all unrighteousness.*"

   Some of us remember when we first heard this Word. When it came, it was to us like the clear shining after rain: "But there is forgiveness." Some of us were, perhaps, for weeks and months without any knowledge of this blessed truth of God—pining for it, hungering for it—and when the Lord brought it home with power into

---

[61] Charles Spurgeon, There is Forgiveness, Public Domain, 1877, spurgeongems.org/vols40-42/chs2422.pdf., P. 3.

[62] John Gill, *Commentary of the Whole Bible*, Public Domain, 1816, Ibid, P. 303.

[63] Adam Clarke, *The Adam Clarke Commentary Corinthians through Philemon*, Public Domain, 1836, Ibid

our hearts by the Holy Spirit, oh, there was no music like it! Angels could not sing any tune so sweet as these Words of God spoken to our hearts by the Holy Spirit.[64]
– Charles Spurgeon

2. <u>God Forgets</u>: Isaiah 43:25, "*I, even I, am he who blots out your transgressions, for my own sake, and remembers your sins no more.*"

Psalm 103:11-12 opens the windows of the universe to reveal its infinite scope and range. "*For as high as the heavens are above the earth, so great is his love for those who fear him; as far as the east is from the west, so far has he removed our transgressions from us.* We see in these two verses God's great love, His mercy for those who believe in Him, and the grace that completely eradicates our sin.

God, in His unsearchable, unmatched love, forgives our sins. Ephesians 1:7 states, "*In him, we have redemption through his blood, the forgiveness of sins, in accordance with the riches of God's grace.*"

His mercy isolates us from what we deserve. Through our disobedient actions, we have earned eternal isolation and suffering at the hand of a righteous God. But God in His unmatched, extraordinary mercy, has freed us from that end.

Finally, our salvation itself is a product of God's grace (Hebrews 2:9). By grace, through faith, God has erased the sin in our lives forever.

The unrighteous actions of the past are gone. The spurious, fractious acts we presently perform are being expunged as they are committed. The disobedient acts that we will perform in the future deleted from our record. We who are guilty but believe have already been sanctified and positionally glorified. We have been freed from sin and death. We have been rescued from eternal punishment because God has forgiven our unrighteousness.

---

[64] Charles Spurgeon, *There is Forgiveness*, Ibid., P. 2.

3. *We Must be like God*:

If God forgives us, we should forgive others. If He forgets our sins how can we not do the same? The pathway to forgiveness is found in the life and actions of Jesus. We must imitate Jesus. Ephesians 5:1-2 states, *"Be imitators of God, therefore, as dearly loved children and live a life of love, just as Christ loved us and gave himself up for us as a fragrant offering and sacrifice to God."*

Spiritual Application

Forgiveness is a two-way street. Our God forgives us unconditionally. We must forgive others in the same way. The impetus for God's forgiveness began with His love for us. We must develop an attitude of love for each other. 1 Peter 4:8 tells us, *"Above all, love each other deeply because love covers over a multitude of sins."*

The first step in forgiveness is learning to love others unconditionally.

Lessons within the Lesson

Why does a God of justice provide for the sin of His children? Read Micah 7:18-19 and Ephesians 1-7-8.

Why won't we be judged for our unrighteous actions past, present, and future? Read Psalm 103:10-12 and Hebrews 2:9.

Since we will not be judged for our disobedient acts, why don't we live a worldly life and forget about righteousness? Read Romans 6:1-7.

What does it mean to be imitators of Christ? Read Philippians 2:3-8 and John 15:9-11.

14. LOVE DOES NOT DELIGHT IN EVIL

Prayer

Lord, our God, don't allow us to enjoy any nonbeliever's misfortune or mishap. In addition, Help us to resist the temptation that comes when we see their disobedient actions. Encourage us to remember, but for the grace of God that could be me, Amen.

Today's Scripture: 1 Corinthians 13:6a

Love does not delight in evil.

Do not gloat when your enemy falls; when he stumbles, do not let your heart rejoice, or the Lord will see and disapprove and turn his wrath away from him. Do not fret because of evil men or be envious of the wicked, for the evil man has no future hope, and the lamp of the wicked will be snuffed out (Proverbs 24:17-20).

Associated Scriptures

Although they know God's righteous decree that those who do such things deserve death, they not only continue to do these very things but also approve of those who practice them (Romans 2:32).

Hatred stirs up conflict, but love covers over all wrongs (Proverbs 10:12).

Above all, love each other deeply, because love covers over a multitude of sins (1 Peter 4:8).

Correlative Quotes

Love makes allowances for the falls of others and is ready to put on them a charitable construction (the face of love). Love, so far from devising evil against another, excuses "the evil" which another inflicts on her [Estius]; does not meditate upon evil inflicted by another

[Bengel]; and in doubtful cases, takes the more charitable view [Grotius].[65] – Jamieson, Fausset, Brown

(There are those who) even weep at either the sin or folly of even an enemy; they take no pleasure in hearing or in repeating it but desire it may be forgotten forever.[66] – John Wesley

See Romans 1:32 for this depth of degradation. There are people as low as that whose real joy is in the triumph of evil.[67] – A. T. Robertson

Author's Notes

INTRODUCTION

It is human nature to enjoy the demise of those who struggle in this world. We see these unfortunate souls are being punished by the very system that drives them farther from God. Life in the world for unbelievers is a continuous rollercoaster. As they fall deeper in love with the fame, the fortune of success, unhealthy sexual activity, or the highs they receive from addictions to habit-forming substances, they seal their own fate. Unfortunately, some Christians suffer from same issues. Many try to live in the world and please God at the same time. It won't work for either group.

Our duty to God requires a response in love. We are not to chide, lecture, or embarrass others. We must show compassion to everyone. Believers should not be judging others. We should not enjoy their outward displays of relentless impatience. The eagerness that consumes them in their struggle. We must be an encouragement to those who struggle so that they would see the love of Christ in us and turn to him for salvation. Our lives must be a witness to others; continually. This is the example of Jesus in our lives (1 Corinthians 11:1).

---

[65] Jamieson, Robert, D. D.; Fausset, A. R.; Brown, David, Commentary Critical and Explanatory on the Whole Bible, Public Domain 1871, Ibid., P. 3560.

[66] John Wesley, *John Wesley's Notes of the Bible*, Public Domain, Publication date 1755, Ibid., P. 320.

[67] A. T. Robertson, New Testament Word Pictures, Public Domain, Ibid, P. 1516.

FOLLOW GOD'S EXAMPLE

Psalm 5:4 tells us, "For you are not a God who delights in wickedness; evil may not dwell with you."

1. <u>Do not Gloat</u>: Proverbs 24:17-18, *"Do not gloat when your enemy falls; when he stumbles, do not let your heart rejoice, or the Lord will see and disapprove and turn his wrath away from him."*

Sin has made mankind enemies of each other. Meaningless, unjustified beliefs cause unwarranted anger. Wrath rules the day. God's plan for man is that we would live in peace, respecting each other as equals (Matthew 7:12). He wants us to love each other and live in unity (Colossians 3:13-14). Diversity has caused the opportunity for derision, mockery, and the bitterness that leads to ridicule.

2. <u>Do not Get Bothered</u>: Proverbs 24:19a, *"Do not fret because of evil men"*

It is amazing what people get upset over. We all see and personally experience this reaction to injustice and unrighteous actions every day. The question that we need to ask ourselves is this, "Do I have any control over the outcome of these issues." In addition, we should ask, "What action can I take in my day to day life that will change the condition that makes me angry."

God does not want us to be bothered or angered by the things in this world over which we have no control. He says in James 1:19-20, *"My dear brothers and sisters, take note of this: Everyone should be quick to listen, slow to speak and slow to become angry, because human anger does not produce the righteousness that God desires."* If we cannot impact a wrong, we must begin to pray that God will. Prayer eliminates anger.

3. <u>Do not Desire what Evil can Offer</u>: Proverbs 24:19b-20, *"(Don't be) envious of the wicked, for the evil man has no future hope, and the lamp of the wicked will be snuffed out."*

The only action worse than emotional anger or its physical response is the fleshly desire to participate in it. Temptation is not sin. However, the desire itself, as it grows, will produce unjustifiable action. James 1:14 explains this issue and its result. *"...but each person is tempted when they are dragged away by their own evil desire and enticed. Then, after desire has conceived, it gives birth to sin; and sin, when it is full-grown, gives birth to death. Don't be deceived, my dear brothers and sisters."* Instead of walking in the desires of the flesh, walk in the Spirit (Galatians 5:16-17).

Spiritual Application

One finds nothing but love where it is real. For circumstances are but an occasion for it to act and show itself. Love is always itself and it is love which is exercised and displayed. It is that which fills the mind: Everything else is but a means of awakening the soul that dwells in love to its exercise (action). This is the divine character. No doubt the time of judgment will come; but our relationships with God are in grace. Love is His nature. It is now the time of its exercise (action). We represent Him on earth in testimony.[68] – John Nelson Darby

Lessons within the Lesson

What does arrogance or pride accomplish for the believer? Read Proverbs 16:18 and 16:5.

How does God react to our arrogance and pride? Read Proverbs 11:2, Proverbs 13:10, and Proverbs 29:23.

How does God want us to react to upsetting situations in life? Read Psalm 100.

What is the antidote for arrogance and pride? Read Philippians 2:5-7.

---

[68] John Nelson Darby, Synopsis of the Books of the Bible, Public Domain, 1857- 62, stempublishing.com/authors/darby/synopsis/. Pp. 128.

15. LOVE REJOICES IN THE TRUTH

Prayer

You are Truth, Oh Lord. Your truth provides the pattern for our righteousness. Guide us, Spirit of God, into a life that is filled with Truth that we may walk in Your light. In Christ's Holy name we pray, Amen!

Today's Scripture: 1 Corinthians 13:6b

Love rejoices in the truth,

Teach me your way, O Lord , and I will walk in your truth; give me an undivided heart, that I may fear your name (Psalms 86:11).

Associated Scriptures

It has given me great joy to find some of your children walking in the truth, just as the Father commanded us (2 John 1:4).

But for those who are self-seeking and who reject the truth and follow evil, there will be wrath and anger (Romans 2:8).

Then you will know the truth, and the truth will set you free (John 8:32).

Correlative Quotes

Exults not at the perpetration of iniquity (unrighteousness) by others (compare Genesis 9:22, 23), but rejoices when the truth rejoices; sympathizes with it in its triumphs (2 John 1:4). See the opposite (2 Timothy 3:8), "Resist the truth." So "the truth" and "unrighteousness" are contrasted (Romans 2:8). "The truth" is the Gospel truth, the inseparable ally of love (Ephesians 4:15; 2 John 1:12). The false charity which compromises "the truth" by glossing over "iniquity" or unrighteousness is thus tacitly condemned (Proverbs 17:15).[69] – Jamieson, Fausset, Brown

(Love) rejoices in the truth - Bringing forth its proper fruit, holiness of heart and life. Good in general is its glory and joy, wherever diffused in all the world.[70] – John Wesley

...but rejoices in the truth; in the truth of the Gospel, and the success of it; such an one can do nothing against it, but for it, will buy it at any rate, but sell it upon no account whatever; and he rejoices greatly when he sees any walking in it."[71] – John Gill

Author's Notes

INTRODUCTION

...when the spiritual life is sound, it produces prayer at the right time and humiliation of soul and sacred joy spring forth spontaneously apart from rules and vows.[72] – Charles Spurgeon

Truth Brings Joy (Psalms 86:11).

Christians experience ultimate joy when they live in God's truth. God's truth gives life. His word shows believers that He is a God of grace, mercy, and love. God's expression of these three characteristics translates into spiritual transformation in the life of the believer. We who have faith in Christ have been resurrected with Jesus. The Spirit has brought life to mankind and made us His children through rebirth. Is it any wonder that "love rejoices in Truth?"

---

[69] Jamieson, Robert, D. D.; Fausset, A. R.; Brown, David, Commentary Critical and Explanatory on the Whole Bible, Public Domain 1871, Ibid., P. 3560.

[70] John Wesley, *John Wesley's Notes of the Bible*, Public Domain, Publication date 1755, Ibid, P. 320.

[71] John Gill, *Commentary of the Whole Bible*, Public Domain, 1816, Ibid, pp. 303-4.

[72] Charles Spurgeon, *Life by Faith*, Public Domain, 1868, liveprayer.com/spurgeon-sermons.cfm?s=187478.

LOVE AND TRUTH

1. Teach Me Your Way, O Lord: Psalms 86:11a

God's way is truth. "Jesus answered, "*I am the way and the truth and the life. No one comes to the Father except through me*" (John 14:6). Jesus doesn't just demonstrate the way; He is the Way. He does only illustrate the truth; Jesus is the Truth. He doesn't uniquely portray the life; Jesus is the Life.

God expects us to live in the way. Living in the way would infer walking in the Spirit. Galatians 5:16 teaches, "*So I say, walk by the Spirit, and you will not gratify the desires of the flesh.*" This would include both living our lives in the way and emulating Jesus in your daily life along the way. It describes a total commitment to living the way God wants us to live.

God also requires us to live according to His truth. Proverbs 30:5 explains that "*Every word of God is flawless; he is a shield to those who take refuge in him.*" God will be a shield, a protector for His children.

Finally, Jesus is the life. Job says in 33:4, "*The Spirit of God has made me, and the breath of the Almighty gives me life.* All people owe life to God. However, it is only Christians that recognize that all life, human life, and spiritual life, come from God.

2. Walk in the Truth: Psalms 86:11b, "*and I will walk in your truth*"

Believers are to walk in the Truth. 1 John 1:7 reveals this truth when it says, "*But if we walk in the light, as he is in the light, we have fellowship with one another, and the blood of Jesus, his Son, purifies us from all sin.*" The light is God's Truth.

3. Focus on God: Psalms 86:11c, "*give me an undivided heart*"

So, let's keep focused on that goal, those of us who want everything God has for us. If any of you have something else in mind, something less than total commitment, God will clear your blurred vision — you'll see it yet (Philippians 3:15 MSG)!

4. Give God the Credit and Glory: Psalms 86:11d, "*that I may fear your name*"

Proverbs 9:10, *"The fear of the LORD is the beginning of wisdom, and knowledge of the Holy One is understanding."*

God is an awesome God (Psalm 68:35). Job 37:23 tells us that God is all-powerful (omnipotence). Isaiah 40:13-14 explains that God knows everything (omniscience). He knows our every thought. Jeremiah 23:23-24 says that God is everywhere at once (omnipresent). God hears every word (Psalm 139:4). He sees every action and reaction. We cannot hide from God.

Christians should be afraid of God. However, this is not the fear of Proverbs 9:10. The beginning of wisdom, knowledge, and understanding comes from reverence to and for God; overwhelming, all-encompassing respect. His children show respect to God by being obedient. We discover obedience through the Word, the Truth of God.

Spiritual Application

The joy of the Lord that comes from walking in His Truth is contagious. First, our walk with God in His Truth gives the trinitarian family joy. Secondly, His Truth in our lives manifests itself as joy in our lives. We find the depth of the joy of God by serving Him. Finally, others see our joy and glorify God. This draws them to want what we are experiencing. This would be called a win, win, win situation.

Lessons within the Lesson

What does Jesus mean when He says in John 14:6, I am the way, the truth, and the light?

How does this truth impact His expectation for believers?

What can we do to be obedient to this expectation?

Describe the overall focus of Psalm 86:11.

16. LOVE ALWAYS PROTECTS

Prayer

I will praise you, LORD, with all my heart; before the "gods" I will sing your praise. I will bow down toward your holy temple and will praise your name for your unfailing love and your faithfulness, for you have so exalted your solemn decree that it surpasses your fame. When I called, you answered me; you greatly emboldened me (Psalm 138:1-3). You are our protector, our shield against the enemy of our souls in this world. We give continued thanks to you, O, Lord, in Christ's precious and Holy Name, we pray, Amen!

Today's Scripture: 1 Corinthians 13:7a

Love always protects (bears all things, ESV, HCSB, NASB, and NKJV).

*He holds victory in store for the **upright**, he is a **shield** to those whose walk is blameless, for he **guards** the course of the just and **protects** the way of his faithful ones. Then you will **understand** what is right and just and fair — every good path* (Proverbs 2:7-9).

Associated Scriptures

For if God did not spare angels when they sinned, but sent them to hell, putting them into gloomy dungeons to be held for judgment; if he did not spare the ancient world when he brought the flood on its ungodly people, but protected Noah, a preacher of righteousness, and seven others; if he condemned the cities of Sodom and Gomorrah by burning them to ashes, and made them an example of what is going to happen to the ungodly; and if he rescued Lot, a righteous man, who was distressed by the filthy lives of lawless men (for that righteous man, living among them day after day, was tormented in his righteous soul by the lawless deeds he saw and heard)—if this is so, then the Lord knows how to rescue godly men from trials and to hold the unrighteous for the day of judgment, while continuing their punishment. This is especially true of those who follow the corrupt desire of the sinful natured and despise authority (2 Peter 2:4-10).

And we know that God causes all things to work together for good to those who love God, to those who are called according to His purpose (Romans 8:28).

He holds success in store for the upright, he is a shield to those whose walk is blameless, *He guards the paths of the just and protects those who are faithful to him.* (Proverbs 2:7-8, NLT).

Correlative Quotes

Love covers unworthy things, rather than bringing them to the light and magnifying them (cf. 1 Pet. 4:8). It puts up with everything ("bears all things").[73] – Thomas Constable

(Bears all things) Greek: Steg "is an old verb (meaning) roof, (as) in 1Corinthians 9:12; 1Thessalonians 3:1,5... Love covers, protects, forbears...1Peter 4:8 "because love covers a multitude of sins" ... throws a veil over.[74] – A. T. Robertson

The burdens of fellow Christians, and so fulfils the law of Christ, which is the law of love; the infirmities of weak believers, and the reproaches and persecutions of the world: or "covers all things", as it may be rendered, even

---

[73] Thomas Constable, Expository Notes of Dr. Thomas Constable, Public Domain, planobiblechapel.org/constable-notes/, P. 239.

[74] A. T. Robertson, New Testament Word Pictures Volume 6, this work is in the Public Domain. Copy Freely, Ibid, P. 1516.

a multitude of sins, as charity is said to do.[75] – John Gill

Author's Notes

INTRODUCTION

Most translations of verse 7 of chapter 13 interpret this first phrase as "Bears all things." However, the Greek word would suggest an interpretation of "protects" (NIV) or "provides a covering for all things." The Amplified version renders the text "Love bears up under anything and everything that comes." This seems to be the most accurate conversion of the Greek thought.

God's love will guide us through the most difficult circumstances of life. This is the example we are to follow. Our love for others must support them through the best of conditions and the worst storms of life.

VICTORY AWAITS THE RIGHTEOUS:

1. <u>God is a Shield to those whose Walk is Blameless</u>:

Love exists as a protective cover for us. It "bears all things" in a way that protects us from a world that tests and tempts us. The love of God provides power over temptation to those who turn to Him.

God said of Job, "*Have you considered my servant Job? There is no one on earth like him; he is blameless and upright, a man who fears God and shuns evil.*" Job was a man who was not perfect. As Satan was sifting him (Luke 22:31), Job had many questions for God. However, He never lost faith in God. Job's belief in God never wavered nor did he curse God (Job 2:9-10). Job 2:10b makes this affirmative statement, "*In all this, Job did not sin in what he said.*" Even under the great pressure of total loss, Job remained resolute, his faith anchored in God.

God had set the parameters for Satan's test (Job 2:4-6). The great love that God had for him allowed Job to bear the losses inflicted.

---

[75] John Gill, *Commentary of the Whole Bible,* Public Domain, 1816, preteristarchive.com/ 1816_gill_commentary/, P. 304.

2. God Guards and Protects the Way of His Faithful:

Wisdom will save you from the ways of wicked men, from men whose words are perverse (Proverbs 2:12).

God's wisdom guards and protects the plans and the pathway of those who are in fellowship with Him. God expects us to step out in faith. His plans for us require risk. Executing God's plan for our lives will expose us to ridicule, sacrifice, and suffering. However, the pathway of risk leads to the final reward. Keep your eye on the goal and mind on the prize.

...for I know whom I have believed, and I am convinced that he is able to guard until that day what has been entrusted to me (2 Timothy 1:12).

3. God Shows us what is Right:

His understanding helps us to differentiate right from wrong and justice from injustice. The Holy Spirit lives in us. He convicts us of wrongdoing and puts us back on the right track (John 16:8, ESV). We know what is right and we should live according to that knowledge. Life isn't fair. However, God is always just and righteous.

Spiritual Application

God's love guards us from harm. He cheers us on during the great moments in our lives and consoles us in the sad and lonely times. He provides a shield or hedge around us to guard us against harm. God keeps us close to Himself through His deep and abiding love.

Lessons within the Lesson

How does God's love protect us? Read Proverbs 3:5-6.

How does God's love shield us? Read Psalm 28:7 and Psalm 18:2.

How does God's wisdom cover us? Read Proverbs 4:6.

Explain the link between understanding and wisdom.

Read Proverbs 2.

17. LOVE ALWAYS TRUSTS

Prayer

We cry out to You Oh Lord of glory to give us the assurance of our justification. It is our prayer that You, Oh Spirit of God, would show us Your ways, O Lord, teach us Your paths; guide us in Your truth and teach us, for You are God our Savior, and our hope is in You all day long (Psalms 25:4-5). You, Jesus, are our only promise of salvation. You are our only pathway to eternal life. If we cannot trust in Your life, death, resurrection, and ascension, we cannot trust in anything else. Our trust is solely in You, precious and loving Savior, Amen!

Today's Scripture: 1 Corinthians 13:7b

Love always trusts (believes all things, NASB, NKJV, ESV)

...love is ever ready to believe the best of every person (AMP).

Trust in the LORD with all your heart and lean not on your own understanding; in all your ways submit to him, and he will make your paths straight (Proverbs 3:5-6).

Associated Scriptures

I rejoice that in everything I have confidence in you (2 Corinthians 7;16).

We have confidence in the Lord concerning you, that you are doing and will continue to do what we command (2 Thessalonians 3:4).

We have sent with them our brother, whom we have often tested and found diligent in many things, but now even more diligent because of his great confidence in you (2 Corinthians 8:22).

Correlative Quotes

Believeth all things - Puts the most favorable construction on everything, and is ever ready, to believe whatever may tend to the advantage of any one character.[76] – John Wesley

Love believeth all things — not that the Christian knowingly and willingly allows himself to be imposed upon — not that he divests himself of prudence and judgment, that he may be the more easily taken advantage of — not that he unlearns the way of distinguishing black from white. What then? He requires here, as I have already said, simplicity and kindness in judging of things; and he declares that these are the invariable accompaniments of love.[77] – John Calvin

Believes all things: Is ever ready to believe the best of every person and will credit no evil of any but on the most positive evidence...[78] – Adam Clarke

Author's Notes

INTRODUCTION

It is very difficult, in this age, to trust anyone. Many people today would rather lie than tell the truth. This is a negative way to look at life. We have all lied. We are all guilty before God. Begin looking at life through God's eyes and not the eyes of mankind.

I asked my dad long ago, "How can you trust anyone." His answer was short and thought-provoking yet at the same time insightful. He said, "Trust each and every person until they break that trust. That was an important lesson. It has served me well over my many years. It has worked well with friends, employees, and

---

[76] John Wesley, *John Wesley's Notes of the Bible*, Public Domain, Publication date 1755, Ibid. P. 320.

[77] John Calvin, *Commentaries on the Catholic Epistles*, Rights: Public Domain, Ibid., P. 264.

[78] Adam Clarke, *The Adam Clarke Commentary Corinthians through Philemon*, Public Domain, © 1836, Ibid, P. 142-143.

associates. Remember our own condition before we judge others.

My father's statement mirrors what God says in 1 Corinthians 13:7, the Amplified Version, "...*love is ever ready to believe the best of every person*" (AMP).

A TURN OF EVENTS

This statement in 1 Corinthians 13:7, "Love always trusts," represents a slap in the face or wakeup call to the Corinthian church. Paul had established the Church at Corinth on his first missionary journey. Not long after the formation of the church, Paul received news about the conflicts in Corinth and questions from the church. He answered their concerns in 1 Corinthians 14-16.

When the original letter to the church was delivered, it was not received well. This is also true of Paul's second trip to Corinth. He was met with anger and rejection. Paul left the city dejected and distraught. Before he returned for the third time, Paul sent Titus ahead to take the spiritual temperature of the church. Titus returned after many months with the news that the church had repented and was in good spiritual shape.

The change of heart on the part of the Corinthian Church was amazing. Paul rejoiced at their newfound acceptance of his teaching. The church that had lost Paul's trust had now again become people to be trusted. Trust lost can be regained

TRUSTING

Those who trust in Jesus completely have lives that reflect a total faith in Him.

1. Trusting Believers Reflect Obedience to God: 1 Peter 1:14-16 sets the standard of obedience when Peter writes, "*As obedient children, do not conform to the evil desires you had when you lived in ignorance. But just as he who called you is holy, so be holy in all you do; for it is written: 'Be holy, because I am holy.'*"

   The standard set by God reflects complete obedience. If we believe in God and accept His free gift of salvation, our actions will reflect the trust that accompanies that act of grace.

2. Trusting Believers Reflect God's Love: In Romans 13:8 (ESV)

Paul writes, "*Owe no one anything, except to love each other, for the one who loves another has fulfilled the law.*" To reflect the love of Jesus is to imitate His every act. Christ's love was unconditional love. He did not love us because we earned it, deserved it, or were entitled to it. He loved us because He is love. When we become the love of Christ, then we love as He loved, without restriction.

3. Trusting Believers Reflect God's Joy: John 15:11 explains, "*I have told you this so that my joy may be in you and that your joy may be complete.*" God's joy touches us when we fully trust in Christ. The amazing feeling of euphoria that fills us with the everlasting joy of His presence is indescribable. The wellspring of inner delight lights up our lives and conquers all uncertainty. This joy does not resemble the happiness that the world offers. Happiness comes and goes while the joy of the Lord remains.

4. Trusting Believers Reflect God's Peace: In John 14:27, Jesus tells us, "*Peace I leave with you; my peace I give you. I do not give to you as the world gives. Do not let your hearts be troubled and do not be afraid.*" Philippians 4:7 reveals that "*...the peace of God, which transcends all understanding, will guard your hearts and your minds in Christ Jesus.*" God's peace "*transcends*," goes beyond, surpasses, all of our "*understanding*". We cannot comprehend His great peace. We live lives filled with unrest and doubt. Yet, when we pray, receive, and rest in His pure peace, we feel comfort that cannot found elsewhere in this world.

John says; don't let anxiety rule your life. Instead of fear that leads to hopelessness, God's peace will fill us with His Spirit. We will experience the fruits of the Spirit to their fullest (Galatians 5:22-23). We will learn, through His Spirit, greater trust in Him. That trust will give us whole and complete assurance and trust.

5. Trusting Believers Reflect God's Patience: David wrote in Psalm 145:8, "*The LORD is gracious and compassionate, slow to anger and rich in love.*" We have a Savior who is patient and slow to become angry. Because He is "rich in love," God is worthy of our trust.

Trust and patience go hand-in-hand. In Colossians 1:9-11, Paul and his disciples pray for the church at Colossi that they might trust completely in God and be strengthened with *"endurance and patience."* *"...we have not stopped praying for you and asking God to fill you with the knowledge of his will through all spiritual wisdom and understanding. ...that you may live a life worthy of the Lord and may please him in every way...being strengthened with all power according to his glorious might so that you may have great endurance and patience..."* Paul was asking them to trust in their conversion experience and that their trust would lead to even greater patience. Patience, in this context, becomes a product of spiritual growth.

6. <u>Trusting Believers Reflect God's Kindness</u>: Ephesians 2:6-7, *"And God raised us up with Christ and seated us with him in the heavenly realms in Christ Jesus, in order that in the coming ages he might show the incomparable riches of his grace, expressed in his kindness to us in Christ Jesus."*

   We often focus on the sacrifice of Christ in taking on a human body (Philippians 2:6-7) and then dying for our iniquities (Philippians 2:8). Rightly So. This was truly an act of incredible, unimaginable kindness. However, there was another equal or maybe greater sacrifice in that God allowed it to happen. Both were monumental acts of grace and kindness toward mankind. Christ made the sacrifice that we could not pay. God allowed it to happen and then offered it to us as a free gift of grace (Ephesians 2:8-9). These gifts of a life for the lives of mankind and the grace that brought us eternal life can only be viewed as the greatest acts of kindness in the history of eternity itself.

7. <u>Trusting Believers Reflect God's Goodness</u>: The current adage says, "God is Good." The response is "All the time!" There is an abundance of scripture to substantiate these statements. Psalms 34:8 says, *"Taste and see that the Lord is good."* The psalmist in Psalm 119:68 reflects, *"You are good, and what you do is good."* Lamentations 3:23 explains, *"The Lord is good to those whose hope is in him, to the one who seeks him."* In Mark 10:18, Jesus makes this statement, *"No one is good — except God alone."* God is Good and since He is God, His goodness is eternal.

8. Trusting Believers Reflect God's Self-Control: Proverbs 29:11 explains, *"A fool always loses his temper, But a wise man holds it back."* In the five stages of spiritual growth, knowledge, understanding, wisdom, application, and transformation, wisdom allows us to see clearly what needs to be applied to our lives. The application stage actually produces the anticipated change in behavior. God gives us the wisdom that defines the action required to control our emotions. The application is the action taken.

Spiritual Application

Our relationship with God is built on trust. Proverbs 3:5 tells us to *"Trust in the Lord with all your heart and lean not on your own understanding."* Even though trust is the essential foundation of our connection to God, the continual action of trust and the emulation of God's characteristics are critical to our growth as Christians and our ongoing close relationship with Him. Trust is a verb.

Lessons within the Lesson

Who can we trust? Read Psalm 56:10-13.

What is the basis for actions that would mirror the love of God? See Galatians 5:22

From the list of God's actions of trust, identify one Godly action that the Spirit has directed you to perform.

How do we build trust that leads others to see God? Reread Proverbs 3:5-6

18. LOVE ALWAYS HOPES

Prayer

Show me your ways, O Lord, teach me your paths; guide me in your truth and teach me, for you are God my Savior, and my hope is in you all day long. Remember, O Lord, your great mercy and love, for they are from of old (Psalms 25:4-6). In Christ's name, we pray, Amen!

Today's Scripture: 1 Corinthians 13:7c

Love always hopes

...the testing of your faith produces perseverance. Let perseverance finish its work so that you may be mature and complete, not lacking anything (James 1:3-4).

Associated Scriptures

One whose hope is in you will ever be put to shame (Psalms 25:3).

We know that the whole creation has been groaning as in the pains of childbirth right up to the present time. Not only so, but we ourselves, who have the firstfruits of the Spirit, groan inwardly as we wait eagerly for our adoption as sons, the redemption of our bodies. For in this hope we were saved. But hope that is seen is no hope at all. Who hopes for what he already has? But if we hope for what we do not yet have, we wait for it patiently (Romans 8:22-25).

Be joyful in hope, patient in affliction, faithful in prayer (Romans 12:12).

Correlative Quotes

What a heaven this will be! I think, if I could be sure of getting free from every liability to sin, I would not have a choice as to where I should live, whether on earth or in heaven, at the bottom of the sea with Jonah, or in the low dungeon with Jeremiah. Purity is peace—holiness is happiness. He who is holy as God is holy will in consequence be happy as God is happy. This is one main object of our hope. The other object of our desire is the redemption of the body.[79] – Charles Spurgeon

it (Love) will judge well, and believe well, as far as it can with any reason, and will rather stretch its faith beyond appearances for the support of a kind opinion; but it will go into a bad one with the upmost reluctance, and fence against it as much as it fairly and honestly can. And when, in spite of inclination, it cannot believe well of others, it will yet hope well, and continue to hope as long as there is any ground for it.[80] – Matthew Henry

…victory over death (which is no barrier to this life); and, at the same time, the strengthening and establishment of hope in our common departure, similarly to that of Jesus, (means) to be forever with Him.[81] – John Nelson Darby

Author's Notes

INTRODUCTION

God never intended for us to experience stress, grief, anguish, and suffering. His plan was for us to live forever, in paradise, serving and worshiping Him. However, we chose to be disobedient to God. As a result, instead of the God of the Universe, we serve the god of this world (John 3:19). We cannot serve two masters (Matthew 6:24 and John 16:13).

---

[79] Charles Spurgeon, " Saved in Hope, Public Domain, 1881, spurgeongems.org/vols25-27/chs1616.pdf. P. 4.

[80] Matthew Henry, *Matthew Henry Concise Commentary on the Whole Bible (Unabridged)*, Volume VI (Acts to Revelation), Public Domain, 1706, Ibid, P. 819.

[81] John Nelson Darby, Synopsis of the Books of the Bible, Public Domain, 1857- 62, stempublishing.com/authors/darby/synopsis/.

Through salvation, hope gives us the security to believe that God is in control regardless of our physical, emotional, or financial position in the world. The world does not love us; God does.

But, most people in their current condition, face problems so deep and devastating that many suffer from daily depression. We have problems at home, with our offspring, in our marriages, and yes even in our churches.

People place their hope in earthly things and in other people instead of an eternal God. Just as there is no salvation outside of faith in Jesus Christ, there is no hope outside of an ongoing relationship with God

FIVE BIBLICAL TRUTHS LEADING TO HOPE

Romans 5:1-5 (NKJV) teaches us that *"Therefore, having been justified by faith, we have peace with God through our Lord Jesus Christ, through whom also we have access by faith into this grace in which we stand, and rejoice in hope of the glory of God. And not only that, but we also glory in tribulations, knowing that tribulation produces perseverance; and perseverance, character; and character, hope. now hope does not disappoint, because the love of God has been poured out in our hearts by the Holy Spirit who was given to us."*

The question for all of us is: "How do we experience hope on a daily basis?" Just as faith ignites and renews our relationship with God daily, hope gives us the inner strength and assurance to manage the trials we face each day. Hope also encourages us as we look forward to the future.

Romans 5:1-5 outlines five biblical truths that will elevate us from Hopelessness to Hope. The first truth is found in verses 1-2. Since we have been justified by grace through faith we have *"peace with God."* We were promised this peace by Jesus. In John 14:27 He says, *"Peace I leave with you; my peace I give you. I do not give to you as the world gives. Do not let your hearts be troubled and do not be afraid."* We have received God's peace through the indwelling of the Holy Spirit (1 Corinthians 3:16). As a result, we don't need to be afraid of the trappings of this world.

Verses 3a explains the second truth. Since we are new creatures in Christ Jesus (2 Corinthians 5:17), we "rejoice" in our adversities. The peace that dwells in us allows us to "glory" in our trials, grief, heartache, and misfortune: We rejoice in our sufferings (Luke 6:23). The Greek word translated tribulation means pressure.[82] The word which is generally translated "tribulation" or "suffering," refers to the pressures of this world.

The concept that tribulation creates perseverance describes the third biblical truth. Spiritual growth is always the goal. We will grow through determination (vs. 3b). Perseverance, as used here means determination. It represents our ability to withstand difficulties without concession. When we continually rejoice and seek God's grace persistently through times of difficulty the result is perseverance.

Perseverance produces good character (vs. 4a). Character means the proof or testing of something. This phrase explains the fourth truth; endurance causes modification. As runners push beyond their current state of comfort, they reach new levels of endurance. The tenacity to eclipse the norm brings about growth. It is the experience that comes with perseverance produces Character

The final truth comes in vs. 5. Through good and acceptable character, we realize hope. Because God provided salvation in Christ, and because He is the source of all the believer's expectations, He is called the "God of hope." "Hope does not disappoint" (VS. 5) - does not make us ashamed.

IMPORTANT OF HOPE

The hope that we experience in Jesus will never disappoint us. There are many expressions of Hope in the lives of believers.

1. The HOPE of our Salvation: Acts 4:12 (NKJV): ...*for there is no other name under heaven given among men by which we must be saved.*" Jesus is it. There is no other hope of eternal life. There is no hope for life after death. If Jesus is not Lord. If He is not raised from the dead, we are still in our sin. Death is our final

---

[82] James Strong, *Strong's Exhaustive Concordance*, Ibid, P. 169.

act. But in Jesus, we have hope of eternity. This security comes from Christ own words, " (John 14:6, NKJV), "Jesus said to him, *'I am the way, the truth, and the life. No one comes to the Father except through Me."*

2. <u>Hope in our Time of Need</u>: Hebrews 4:15-16 (NKJV) tells us, *"For we do not have a High Priest who cannot sympathize with our weaknesses, but was in all points tempted as we are, yet without sin. Let us, therefore, come boldly to the throne of grace, that we may obtain mercy and find grace to help in time of need."*

Jesus understands our suffering. He suffered humiliation (Mark 14:63-65), punishment (Isaiah 52:14), and even death (John 19:30). Jesus knows our sorrow (Matthew 26:38). He wept over Lazarus' death (John 11:35), He wept over what Jerusalem had become (Luke 19:41), and in the garden (Hebrews 5:7). He understands our pain. Therefore, He can comfort us through the process. 2 Corinthians 1:3-4 tells us, "Blessed be the God and Father of our Lord Jesus Christ, the Father of mercies and God of all comfort, who comforts us in all our affliction so that we will be able to comfort those who are in any affliction with the comfort with which we ourselves are comforted by God."

3. <u>The HOPE of Eternal Life</u>: 2 Corinthians 4:17-18 *"For our light and momentary troubles are achieving for us an eternal glory that far outweighs them all. So, we fix our eyes not on what is seen, but on what is unseen. For what is seen is temporary, but what is unseen is eternal."*

Romans 5:5 makes the declaration, *"hope does not disappoint."* When this life on earth with its many joys and ominous sorrows is finished, the hope that has been the mainstay our lives, that hope will come to fruition. The hope that we seek is the hope of eternal life. It is available only to those who love God with all their heart, soul, and mind and love others with the unconditional love of Jesus. But what a hope it is. "What a day of rejoicing that will be."

Oh, to look beyond death to "the home over there," beyond the swelling flood where souls that were loved of God from before the foundation of the world are safe with Jesus.[83] – Charles Spurgeon

Spiritual Application

THE CIRCLE OF SPIRITUAL GROWTH

The certainty of hope produces spiritual maturity. Spiritual maturity causes greater trust in God. Trust in God motivates our devotion to Christ. Devotion to Christ produces the certainty of Hope. This is the circle of spiritual growth

My hope is built on nothing less,

Than Jesus' blood and righteousness.

I dare not trust the sweetest frame,

But wholly lean on Jesus' name.

On Christ the solid Rock I stand.

All other ground is sinking sand.

All other ground is sinking sand.[84] – Edward Mote

Lessons within the Lesson

Describe what hope means.

Read Hebrews 6:16-20. Why is hope so important to the Christian?

What are some of the things we hope for?

What hope characterizes eternal life? Read 1 Peter 1:3-9.

---

[83] Charles Spurgeon, Vanities and Verities, Public Domain, spurgeongems.org/vols22-24/chs1380.pd., P. 5.

[84] Edward Mote, *My Hope is Built on Nothing Less*, 1863, Public Domain, digitalhymnal.org.htlm.

---

19. LOVE ALWAYS PERSEVERES

Prayer

Be pleased, O Lord, to deliver me; Lord, make haste to help me! Let them be ashamed and brought to mutual confusion who seek to destroy my life; let them be driven backward and brought to dishonor who wish me evil (Psalm 40:13-14, NKJV). Help us, O God, to persevere in the face of those who would destroy us with their actions and words. Protect us from the evil of this world as we grow in You, Amen!

Today's Scripture: 1 Corinthians 13:7d

Love always perseveres

For this very reason, make every effort to add to your faith goodness; and to goodness, knowledge; and to knowledge, self-control; and to self-control, perseverance; and to perseverance, godliness; and to godliness, brotherly kindness; and to brotherly kindness, love. For if you possess these qualities in increasing measure, they will keep you from being ineffective and unproductive in your knowledge of our Lord Jesus Christ (2 Peter 1:5-8).

Associated Scriptures

Consider it all joy, my brethren, when you encounter various trials, knowing that the testing of your faith produces endurance. And let endurance have its perfect result, so that you may be perfect and complete, lacking in nothing (James 1:2-4, NASB).

Blessed is a man who perseveres under trial; for once he has been approved, he will receive the crown of life which the Lord has promised to those who love Him (James 1:12, NASB).

Let love be without hypocrisy. Abhor what is evil; cling to what is good. Be devoted to one another in brotherly love; 1give preference to one another bin honor; not lagging behind in diligence, fervent in spirit, serving the Lord; rejoicing in hope, persevering in tribulation, devoted to prayer, contributing to the needs of the saints, practicing hospitality (Romans 12:9-13, NASB)

Correlative Quotes

(Perseverance involves) ...keeping every sense under proper restraints, and never permitting the animal part to subjugate (overpower or defeat) the rational. Bearing all trials and difficulties with an even mind, enduring in all, and persevering through all.[85] – Adam Clarke

Happy the man who has this heavenly fire glowing in his heart, flowing out of his mouth, and diffusing its warmth over all with whom he has to do![86] – Matthew Henry

In the meantime, it endures all things - Whatever the injustice, the malice, the cruelty of men can inflict. He can not only do, but likewise suffer, all things, through Christ who strengthens him.[87] – John Wesley

Author's Notes

INTRODUCTION

Love perseveres. He is longsuffering. 2 Peter 3:9 says, *"The Lord is not slack concerning his promise, as some men count slackness; but is longsuffering to us-ward, not willing that any should perish, but that all should come to repentance."*

THE CONTEXT OF LOVE

---

[85] Adam Clarke, The New Testament of our Lord and Savior Jesus Christ, A Commentary and Critical Notes, Romans to Revelation, T. Mason and G. Lane Publishers, New York, P 880.

[86] Matthew Henry, Matthew Henry Concise Commentary on the Whole Bible (Unabridged), Volume VI, Acts to Revelation, Public Domain, 1706, Ibid, P. 819.

[87] John Wesley, *John Wesley's Notes of the Bible*, Public Domain, 1755, Ibid, P. 320.

The context of 2 Peter 3:9 appears to be focused on children in Christ. These are believers who have not grown in the knowledge and truth of the word. 1 Peter 2:2 demonstrates this truth when it explains, *"Like newborn babies, crave pure spiritual milk, so that by it you may grow up in your salvation."*

1. <u>To Our Faith, Goodness</u>: 2 Peter 1:5a, *"For this very reason, make every effort to add to your faith goodness;"*

In man (goodness) is not a mere passive quality, but the deliberate preference of right to wrong, the firm and persistent resistance of all moral evil, and the choosing and following of all moral good.[88] – Matthew George Easton

It is by God's grace, through His gift of faith that we are rescued from spiritual death (Ephesians 2:8). Faith battles with the flesh (Romans 7:22-23). The war being waged is a spiritual war (Galatians 5:16-17). To have victory over the flesh we must turn to Jesus. The answer is the cross. Jesus paid the price. The victory, positional sanctification, is already won through justification. However, progressive Christian transformation must be accomplished through the action of application. Therefore, we must apply goodness, the work of the Spirit (Galatians 5:22-23), to our faith to begin and continue the spiritual growth process.

2. <u>To Goodness, Knowledge</u>: 2 Peter 1:5b, *"and to goodness, knowledge;"*

You may learn the doctrines of the Bible, …You may understand the precepts in the letter of them, and the promises in their outward wording, but neither precept nor promise do you truly know until you know the God from whose lips they fell. The knowledge of God is at once the beginning and the end of wisdom.[89] – Charles Spurgeon

---

[88] Matthew George Easton, Illustrated Bible Dictionary, Third Edition, published by Thomas Nelson, 1897, Public Domain, ntslibrary.com/PDF%20Books/Eastons%20Bible%20 Dictionary.pdf, (copy freely) P. 500.

[89] Charles Spurgeon, *Heart-Knowledge of God*, 1874, Public Domain, spurgeon.org/resource-library/sermons/heart-knowledge-of-god#flipbook/, P. 1.

The greatest truth that a person can possess with the mind or learn through experience is God's Truth (Psalms 46:10; John 8:31-32). This cannot be gained by unaided human reason (Job 11:7; Romans 11:33). It is acquired only as God shows Himself to man in nature and conscience (Psalms 19; Romans 1:19-20); in history or providence (Deuteronomy 6:20-25; Daniel 2:21); and especially in the Bible (Psalms 119; Revelation 1:1-3).

Leviticus 11:44-45, *"For I am the LORD your God Consecrate yourselves therefore, and be holy, for I am holy. And you shall not make yourselves unclean with any of the swarming things that swarm on the earth. 'For I am the LORD who brought you up from the land of Egypt to be your God; thus, you shall be holy, for I am holy.'"* God's standard for moral purity is high. Nothing but complete compliance to and with God will suffice.

Moral goodness or virtue must become the foundation of our search for knowledge. As babes in Christ, we learn just as children acquire knowledge. We are taught. In the case of believers, our teacher is the Spirit of God and our textbook is the Bible. Knowledge becomes the foundation for all spiritual growth.

3. <u>To Knowledge, Self-Control</u>: 2 Peter 1:6a, *"and to knowledge, self-control;"*

Like a city whose walls are broken down is a man who lacks self-control (Proverbs 25:28).

Self-control can be defined as the willpower to hold back on the undesirable actions of life. This restraint of inappropriate actions, although possible for a short period of time, cannot be a permanent action in unbelievers. self-discipline requires a higher power. The power to resist temptation is found in the Spirit of God.

4. <u>To Self-Control, Perseverance</u>: 2 Peter 1:6b, *"and to self-control, perseverance;"*

So, do not throw away your confidence; it will be richly rewarded. You need to persevere so that when you have done the will of God, you will receive what he has promised (Hebrews 10:35-36).

Self-control is the basis for perseverance. The Hebrews passage is saying that if believers have confidence in Christ this will allow them to exercise control over their feelings and actions to the point of persevering in times of great difficulty.

The best way to escape from our sufferings is, to be willing to understand that they will endure as long as God pleases." – John Wesley

Perseverance pushes us forward under the most difficult of circumstances. The more ominous and perilous the occasion of our struggle in the process, the greater the reward of growth in the end.

Believers struggle with temptation. Before we became new creatures in Christ, there existed no choice but evil (Romans 3:10-11). Before salvation, we could accomplish nothing good in the eyes of God (Isaiah 64:6). However, once we became a new creation the sin nature died but the free will of man did not. At the point of salvation, God gave us the opportunity to choose good or evil.

As difficult as it is to resist temptation, if we persevere until the suffering subsides or the anguish is overcome, we will receive the reward of victory in this life and a crown of glory in the next. James 1:12 says it in these terms, *"Blessed is a man who perseveres under trial; for once he has been approved, he will receive the crown of life which the Lord has promised to those who love Him."*

Victory over the trials of this world comes from perseverance. It allows us to withstand even the most difficult times and circumstances of life. Perseverance comes from the power and presence of the Holy Spirit (Proverbs 3:5-6).

5. To Perseverance, Godliness: 2 Peter 1:6c, *"and to perseverance, godliness;"*

Let us not lose heart in doing good, for in due time we will reap if we do not grow weary (Galatians 6:9).

Godliness is our victory through perseverance. God uses

trials to stretch our faith. Each time we persist in our faith and allow the Spirit to work in our lives, we move closer to Godliness and the God we love and serve takes us to a new level of assurance and hope. Hope never disappoints us (Romans 5:5).

6. To Godliness, Brotherly Kindness: 2 Peter 1:7a (NASB), *"and in your godliness, brotherly kindness,"*

We cannot be unkind when being prompted to love by the Spirit of God. Godliness causes kindness to others. Sincerity is the key to being kind. 2 Corinthians 1:12 explains that we have conducted our relationships with integrity and godly sincerity. This is the reality of kindness. Acting in truth pleases God.

7. To Brotherly Kindness, Love: 2 Peter 1:7b, *"and in your brotherly kindness, love."*

The result of kindness is love. Love expressed through the Spirit is always unconditional. Unconditional love is never confused with provisional love by the person who receives it.

Spiritual Application

2 Peter 1:5-8 with its seven actions leading to perfect love gives us the essence of spiritual growth. Each of these steps is a powerful reminder of the path that we must take to survive in a world that would attempt to separate us from the love of Jesus.

Lessons within the Lesson

How important is faith in the spiritual growth process? Read Philippians 1:6.

How does self-control bring about persistence?

Explain the importance of persistence. Read Romans 5:3-5.

How does persistence impact Godliness?

20. LOVE NEVER FAILS

Prayer

Give thanks to the LORD, for he is good, for his steadfast love endures forever. Give thanks to the God of gods, for his steadfast love endures forever. Give thanks to the Lord of lords, for his steadfast love endures forever (Psalm 136:1-3, ESV). *Give thanks to the God of heaven, for his steadfast love endures forever* (Psalm 136:26, ESV). It is through Christ's never failing love that we Pray, Amen!

Today's Scripture: 1 Corinthians 13:8a

Love never fails

Associated Scriptures

But you, Lord, are a compassionate and gracious God, slow to anger, abounding in love and faithfulness (Psalm 86:15).

But God demonstrates his own love for us in this: While we were still sinners, Christ died for us (Romans 5:8).

Whoever does not love does not know God, because God is love (1 John 4:8).

Correlative Quotes

Love survives everything.[90] – A. T. Robertson

it (love) always holds its place.[91] – Jamison, Fausset, Brown

---

[90] A. T. Robertson, *New Testament Word Pictures Volume 6,* this work is in the Public Domain. Copy Freely, Ibid, P. 1517.

[91] Jamieson, Robert, D. D.; Fausset, A. R.; Brown, David, *Commentary Critical and Explanatory on the Whole Bible*, Public Domain, 1871, Public Domain, Copy Freely, Ibid, P. 3561.

Here we have another excellence of *love* — *that* it endures forever. There is good reason why we should eagerly desire an excellence that will never come to an end.[92] – John Calvin

Author's Notes

INTRODUCTION

God loves because He is love (1 John 4:8).

HIS LOVE NEVER FAILS BECAUSE

1. <u>God's Truth is Absolute</u>: John 3:33, "Whoever receives his (Christ's) testimony sets his seal to this, that God is true."

   "*What is truth?*", is an age-old question. Mankind has searched for truth since the beginning of time. In John 8:37-38 Jesus answers Pilate's statement, "*You are a King then!*", by explaining that it was His purpose to come into the world to testify to the truth. Pilate inquires cynically, "*What is truth?*" The world teaches moral relativism. Relative truth believes that all moral principles are based on the point of view of the one holding it. Therefore, all moral beliefs are true.

   God's truth is absolute. God himself defines truth. Truth is anything that is consistent with the nature and person of God.

2. <u>God Does Not Change</u>: Malachi 3:6, For I, the LORD, do not change...

   I knew that I could not keep myself, but if Christ promised to keep me, then I should be safe forever.[93] – Charles Spurgeon

   Since God does not change, His love remains constant. Jeremiah 31:3 reads, "*The LORD appeared to us in the past, saying: 'I have loved you with an everlasting love; I have drawn you with unfailing kindness.'*"

   The immutability of God is our absolute guarantee of His

---

[92] John Calvin, *Commentaries on the Catholic Epistles*, Rights: Public Domain, Ibid.

[93] Charles Spurgeon, *Spurgeon Quotes*, Public Domain, princeofpreachers.org/quotes/category/love-of-christ. P. 1

everlasting love. Since God does not change, His love is unalterable. We can always be sure of the nature of God. We also have the assurance through His word in Romans 8:38-39 that "nothing in all of God's creation," or "any other created thing" (HSCB), *"will be able to separate us from the love of God that is in Christ Jesus our Lord."*

3. <u>God is Good</u>: Psalm 100:5, *"For the LORD is good and his love endures forever; his faithfulness continues through all generations."*

   This is true faith, a living confidence in the goodness of God.94 – Martin Luther

   God's goodness reflects His everlasting love for us. He is continually good to us and for us. It is God's grace that brought us salvation (Titus 3:4-6). His kindness provides for our needs (Matthew 7:11). God protects His followers from the evil of this world (Psalm 23:4). Finally, He perseveres us until the time of our resurrection and for an eternity to follow (Psalm 121:8).

4. <u>God is Wholly Merciful</u>: Psalm 51:1-2, *"Have mercy on me, O God, according to your steadfast love; according to your abundant mercy blot out my transgressions. Wash me thoroughly from my iniquity and cleanse me from my sin!"*

   God's mercy can easily be described as *"When we don't get what we do deserve."* We deserve eternal separation from God and punishment. We have all fallen short of the glory of God (Romans 3:23). However, in Christ's single act of unmerited love, He paid the price for our iniquity and provided the free gift of eternal life.

5. <u>God is Unquestionably Faithful</u>: Hebrews 6:16-19, *"Men swear by someone greater than themselves, and the oath confirms what is said and puts an end to all argument. Because God wanted to make the unchanging nature of his purpose very clear*

---

[94] Martin Luther, *Faith is a busy, living, active, mighty thing,* tollelege.wordpress.com/2011/02/11/faith-is-a-living-busy-active-mighty-thing-by-martin-luther/, Public Domain.

to the heirs of what was promised, he confirmed it with an oath. God did this so that, by two unchangeable things in which it is impossible for God to lie, we who have fled to take hold of the hope offered to us may be greatly encouraged. We have this hope as an anchor for the soul, firm and secure."

Salvation for His children is the product of God's love. His faithfulness provides an anchor for the love God transfers to us. His love was expressed through the death and resurrection of Jesus. There is no love greater than this love.

Spiritual Application

Three things God cannot do. He cannot die. He cannot lie, and He cannot be deceived.[95] – Charles Spurgeon

Everything on earth will end someday and a new Heaven and earth will take its place (Revelation 21:1). Pain and suffering will cease. The dishonest, the violent, thieves, and murderers, and all liars will not survive (Revelation 21:8). Disobedience, the product of unrighteousness, will be a thing of the past, never to haunt mankind again. Love will rule the day. Love will survive the holocaust that precedes eternity with God. We know this since love never fails.

Lessons within the Lesson

What can we say about God's truth? Read Psalm 25:5 and Psalm 26:3.

How does God's mercy relate to His Love? Read Psalm 40:11 and Psalm 51:1.

How is God good to us? For us?

Explain the faithfulness of God in relationship to His love.

---

[95] Charles Spurgeon, *Eternal Faithfulness Unaffected by Human Belief*, Public Domain, spurgeongems.org/vols25-27/chs1453.pdf, P. 5

21. PROPHECIES WILL CEASE

Prayer

Turn to me and have mercy on me, as you always do to those who love your name. Direct my footsteps according to your word; let no sin rule over me. Redeem me from the oppression of men, that I may obey your precepts. Make your face shine upon your servant and teach me your decrees (Psalms 119:132-136). Amen!

Today's Scripture: 1 Corinthians 13:8b

Where there are prophecies, they will cease

Associated Scriptures

"On that day, I will banish the names of the idols from the land, and they will be remembered no more," declares the Lord Almighty. *"I will remove both the prophets and the spirit of impurity from the land* (Zechariah 13:2-4).

*Sanctify them by the truth; **your word is truth*** (John 17:17).

*So, faith comes from hearing, and hearing through **the word of Christ*** (Romans 10:17).

Correlative Quotes

A fountain—The source of mercy in Christ Jesus; perhaps referring to the death he should die, and the piercing of his side, when blood and water issued out.[96] – Adam Clarke

Thy word is truth.—There is a strong emphasis in the

---

[96] Adam Clarke, *The Adam Clarke Commentary Corinthians through Philemon*, Vol. 4, Public Domain, © 1836, Ibid, P. 1578.

pronoun "Word is truth." This word they had kept (verses 1-8). It had become the region of their life. They are to be the channels through which it is to pass to others (ver.se 20). **So, have I also sent them into the world**. Better, I also sent. In the very word "Apostles " their mission was contained; but the thought here comprehends (explains) the immediate future of their mission.[97] – Charles Ellicott

(The Scriptures) in the counsel of peace among other things it was settled and agreed. That all needful truth should be comprised and summed up in the word of God. Divine revelation, as it now stands in the written word, is not only pure truth without mixture, but entire truth without deficiency.[98] – Matthew Henry

Author's Notes

INTRODUCTION

The proof of textual applicability belongs to the permanency and immutability of Scripture itself. The amazing fact of the truth of God not only rests in the Word's stability by its currency. God's truth has always been and will always be applicable to current life situations. Hebrews 4:12 explains, "For the word of God is living and active, …discerning the thoughts and intentions of the heart. God's word is relevant to today and it will continue to be pertinent in the future.

God's word grows deeper in its meaning and application as the believer grows and is being transformed. Scriptures that had meaning to us as children in age or in spiritual infancy now have a deeper meaning as we mature and need broader and more profound answers for continued growth. Hebrews 5:14-15 clarifies

---

[97] C. J. Ellicott, (Charles John), *A New Testament Commentary for English Readers*, Vol. 2, 1819-1905. Public Domain, 1897, Ibid, P. 524.

[98] Matthew Henry, Matthew Henry Concise Commentary on the Whole Bible (Unabridged), Volume V (Job to Song of Solomon), Public Domain, 1706, bitimage.dyndns. org/, Pp. 2014-2015

this thought when it says, *"Now everyone who lives on milk is inexperienced with the message about righteousness, because he is an infant. But solid food is for the mature--for those whose senses have been trained to distinguish between good and evil."*

CESSATION OR NON-CESSATION

The key to understanding this argument is found in 1 Corinthians 13:9-12 where we read, *"For we know in part and we prophesy in part, but when perfection comes, the imperfect disappears. When I was a child, I talked like a child, I thought like a child, I reasoned like a child. When I became a man, I put childish ways behind me. Now we see but a poor reflection as in a mirror; then we shall see face to face. Now I know in part; then I shall know fully, even as I am fully known."*

The theme of these verses is cessation. It cannot be argued that the gift of prophecy will not cease. The verse clearly states that it will. The question of cessation is not will it cease but when.

There has been a longstanding argument on both sides of this issue. However, the majority of cessationists fall into three camps. These groups include, but are not limited to, those who believe that prophecy ended with the Apostolic Age. The second group has concluded that prophecy continues in a limited form through the interpretation of scripture. The final group feels that prophecy has always existed and continues in its historical form. All three groups agree that prophetic utterance will not be necessary after the return of Christ in Glory. Thus, everyone agrees in the ultimate cessation of this gift in the future.

1. Prophecy Ended with the Apostolic Age:

Those who believe in early cessation mark it either at the end of the Apostolic Age with the death of the last Apostle John. One of the leading advocates promoting the cessation of miracles at the end of the Apostolic age was B. B. Warfield.

How long did this state of things continue? It was the characterizing peculiarity of specifically the Apostolic Church, and it belonged therefore exclusively to the Apostolic age—although no doubt this designation may be taken with some latitude. These gifts were not the possession of the primitive Christian as such; nor for that matter of the Apostolic Church or the Apostolic age for themselves; they were distinctively the authentication of the Apostles. They were part of the credentials of the Apostles as the authoritative agents of God in founding the church.[99] – B. B. Warfield

2. Limited Prophecy Still Continues:

The next group involved in this discussion believes that the gift of prophecy still exists in a limited form today. These believers restrict prophecy to the interpreting of the mysteries of scripture. This interpretation limits prophesy to the teaching and preaching of biblical truths that already exist.

These Christians hold that this gift will be ongoing until the second coming of Christ when he sets up His Millennial Kingdom on earth. At this point, there will be no need for prophecy since Jesus will be on the throne speaking directly to us as He governs and executes His will directly.

According to their understanding of scripture, the gifts partially ceased at the end of the Apostolic Age. They have determined that all prophecy today is limited to the interpretation of scripture and its application to the believer's life. Some believe that the cessation took place at the final compiling of the scriptures (397 A. D., upon the completion of the Council of Carthage), and exist today in the form of interpretation of Scripture. John Calvin makes this point when he writes,

Let it be observed that two things are here connected, the word and the spirit of God, in opposition to fanatics, who aim at oracles and hidden revelations without (outside of) the word.[100] – John Calvin

---

[99] Benjamin B. Warfield, *Counterfeit Miracles*, Public Domain, 1919, monergism.com/thethreshold/sdg/warfield/warfield_counterfeit.html.

[100] John Calvin, *Commentary on Isaiah*, Quote is Public Domain, rtc.edu.au/RTC/media/Documents/Vox%20articles/Prophecy-in-the-Reformed-Tradition-BB-60-1995.

3. Historic Prophecy Still Exists Today:

The Bible clearly teaches that we are living in the last days. This truth is substantiated by Peter in 1Peter 1:18-20, by John in 1 John 2:18-19, Hebrews 1:1-2, and Mark 1:15. The description of these days hits all to close to home to deny it, *"This know also, that in the last days perilous times shall come. For men shall be lovers of their own selves, covetous, boasters, proud, blasphemers, disobedient to parents, unthankful, unholy, without natural affection, trucebreakers, false accusers, incontinent, fierce, despisers of those that are good, traitors, heady, high-minded, lovers of pleasures more than lovers of God; having a form of godliness, but denying the power thereof: from such turn away. For of this sort are they which creep into houses, and lead captive silly women laden with sins, led away with divers* (different, certain) *lusts, ever learning, and never able to come to the knowledge of the truth* (2 Timothy 3:1-7, KJV).

Many Christians believe that the gift of prophecy remains intact today as it has throughout history. Terms such as special, progressive, or continuous revelation are used by those who believe that God has not completed scripture and He is still adding to biblical truth. However, since 397 A.D. nothing, not one word, has been added to the original texts written by the prophets and apostles. This would be clear evidence that prophecy, as it existed in the Old and New Testaments, has ceased.

A second camp also believes that God still speaks new truth to mankind. However, that truth does not rise to the level of the prophets and apostles. These inspirations are worthy of expression but not given as universal truth for all mankind. As a result, these prophecies do not rise to the level of scripture.

Finally, some theologians would deny any prophecy regardless of the definition or intention. They teach that the word "revelation," as used in the new testament, always means scriptural revelation. 1 Corinthians 14:26 tells us, *"When you come together, each of you has a hymn, or a word of instruction, a revelation, a tongue or an interpretation. Everything must be done so that the church may be built up."* This verse would indicate that messages from God can come to those within the congregation. In addition, these "words from God" are meant to edify (enlighten or buildup) other believers. 1 Thessalonians 5:11says, *"Therefore encourage one another and build each other up, just as in fact you are doing."*

Spiritual Application

With the gift of prophecy, if it exists in any form today, comes a warning in 1John 4:1, *"Dear friends, do not believe every spirit, but test the spirits to see whether they are from God, because many false prophets have gone out into the world."*

> ...the doctrine of the Church in Sermons, and the decrees of councils, are both the word of God and the word of man: The word of God, as it agrees with the writings of the Apostles and Prophets: the word of man, as it is defective, and as it is propounded in terms devised by man.[101] – William Perkins

Lessons within the Lesson

Explain the word prophecy as it pertains to a work of the Spirit?

Make a biblical case for prophecy having ceased at the end of the Apostolic Era. See 2 Corinthians 2:12, Acts 2:43, 5:12, Romans 15:18-19, and Matthew 16:4.

Make a biblical case for the teaching of "limited prophecy." See James 5:14-15, 1 Corinthians 12:9, 13:2, and 1 Timothy 4:14.

What is progressive prophecy and is it from God?

---

[101] William Perkins, The Works of that Famous and Worthy Minister of Christ in the University of Cambridge, the Second Volume (London: John Legatt, 1631), 167

22. TONGUES WILL BE STILLED

Prayer

Forgive my hidden faults, Oh, LORD. Keep your servant also from willful sins; may they not rule over me. Then I will be blameless, innocent of great transgression. May these words of my mouth and this meditation of my heart be pleasing in your sight, LORD, my Rock and my Redeemer (Psalm 19:12-14).

Today's Scripture: 1 Corinthians 13:8c

Where there are tongues, they will be stilled.

Associated Scriptures

The heavens are telling of the glory of God; And their expanse is declaring the work of His hands. Day to day pours forth speech, And night to night reveals knowledge. There is no speech, nor are there words; Their voice is not heard. Their line has gone out through all the earth, And their utterances to the end of the world In them He has placed a tent for the sun (Psalm 19:1-4).

When the day of Pentecost came, they were all together in one place. Suddenly a sound like the blowing of a violent wind came from heaven and filled the whole house where they were sitting. They saw what seemed to be tongues of fire that separated and came to rest on each of them. All of them were filled with the Holy Spirit and began to speak in other tonguesa as the Spirit enabled them. Now there were staying in Jerusalem God-fearing Jews from every nation under heaven. When they heard this sound, a crowd came together in bewilderment, because each one heard them speaking in his own language. Utterly amazed, they asked: "Are not all these men who are speaking Galileans? Then how is it that each of us hears them in his own native language (Acts 2:1-8)?

Therefore, let him who speaks in a tongue pray that he may interpret. For if I pray in a tongue, my spirit prays, but my understanding is unfruitful. What is the conclusion then? I will pray with the spirit, and I will also pray with the understanding. I will sing with the spirit, and I will also sing with the understanding. Otherwise, if you bless with the spirit, how will he who occupies the place of the uninformed say "Amen" at your giving of thanks, since he does not understand what you say? For you indeed give thanks well, but the other is not edified. I thank my God I speak with tongues more than you all; yet in the church I would rather speak five words with my understanding, that I may teach others also, than ten thousand words in a tongue (1 Corinthians 14:13-19, NKJV).

If anyone speaks in a tongue, two--or at the most three-- should speak, one at a time, and someone must interpret (1 Corinthians 14:27).

Correlative Quotes

The Corinthians held an exaggerated estimate of the value of gifts such as tongues and prophecy and undervalued the graces of faith and love. Now the Apostle shows that they were thereby preferring the things which are for a time to the graces which are forever.[102] – C. J. Ellicott

The apostle had been speaking of temporary gifts. Supernatural endowments were granted to the Church for a season only. The apostle intimates that there is a gift of richer value and that the time would come when

---

[102] C. J. Ellicott, (Charles John), *A New Testament Commentary for English Readers*, Vol. 2, 1897. Public Domain, P. 339.

these would be bestowed no longer, and when that (love) only would remain.[103] – Joseph S. Excell

Whether there be tongues, they shall cease - One language shall prevail among all the inhabitants of heaven, and the low and imperfect languages of the earth are forgotten.[104] – John Wesley

The miraculous gift of different languages, that soon shall cease, as being unnecessary.[105] – Adam Clarke

Author's Notes

INTRODUCTION

There is no reference to the spiritual gift of speaking in tongues in the Old Testament. In the book of Joel, we see an account of the last days, "*I* (God) *will pour out my Spirit on all people. Your sons and daughters will prophesy, your old men will dream dreams, your young men will see visions. Even on my servants, both men and women, I will pour out my Spirit in those days* (Joel 2:28-29). In this narrative, we see the miracles of prophecies, prophetic dreams, and visions. However, we do not see the miracle of tongues. The phenomena of the "tongues of fire" (Acts 2:1-4) does not appear anywhere else in the Bible either before this occurrence or afterward.

THE MIRACLE OF SPEAKING IN TONGUES

1. Tongues are Powered by the Spirit of God:

It would appear from the evidence of Scripture, that the spiritual gift of speaking in tongues emerged as a New Testament miracle. We see the first mention of the tongues of fire in the Book of Acts.

---

[103] Joseph S. Excell, The Bible Illustrator, Vol. 27, 1 Corinthians Vol. 1, Public Domain, 1849, Anson D. F. Randolph and Company, New York, New York.

[104] John Wesley, *John Wesley's Notes of the Bible*, Public Domain, Publication date 1755, Ibid, P. 320.

[105] Adam Clarke, *The Adam Clarke Commentary Corinthians through Philemon*, Public Domain, 1836, Ibid, P. 143.

When the day of Pentecost came, they were all together in one place. Suddenly a sound like the blowing of a violent wind came from heaven and filled the whole house where they were sitting. They saw what seemed to be tongues of fire **that separated** *and came to rest on* **each of them. All of them were filled** *with* **the Holy Spirit** *and began* **to speak in other tongues** *as* **the Spirit enabled them.** (Acts 2:2-4).

We see several important truths in the account of this miracle that involved everyone who was in the room. First, the event began with a sound from heaven that was like a great windstorm. Either following or accompanying the wind, we see the phenomenon referred to as "tongues of fire."

Wesley says, "That is, small flames of fire. This is all which the phrase, tongues of fire, means. Yet it might intimate God's touching their tongues as it were (together with their hearts) with Divine fire: his giving them such words as were active and penetrating, even as a flaming fire. the gift of speaking in tongues resulted from the power and presence of the Holy Spirit."[106]

According to Jamieson, Brown, and Fausset, "The suddenness, strength, and diffusiveness of the sound strike with deepest awe the whole company, and thus complete their preparation for the heavenly gift. Wind was a familiar emblem of the Spirit (Ezekiel 37:9; John 3:8; 20:22). But this was not a rush of actual wind. It was only a sound "as of" it."[107]

The episode in Acts 2 took place on the day of Pentecost. This miracle of the filling of the Holy Spirit, "tongues of fire" was a sign to those gathered in the upper room. It marked the onset of the Church Age.

---

[106] John Wesley, *John Wesley's Notes of the Bible*, Public Domain, Publication date 1755, Ibid, P. 191.

[107] Jamieson, Robert, D. D.; Fausset, A. R.; Brown, David, Commentary Critical and Explanatory on the Whole Bible, Public Domain 1871, Ibid., P. 3201.

The Holy Spirit was the catalyst for the expression of the gift. The action of this miracle did not originate in the disciples. The "tongues of fire came to rest on each of them."

2. Tongues are Languages

Now there were staying in Jerusalem God-fearing Jews from every nation under heaven. When they heard this sound, a crowd came together in bewilderment, because each one heard them speaking in his own language. Utterly amazed, they asked: "Are not all these men who are speaking Galileans? Then how is it that each of us hears them in his own native language (Acts 2:5-8)?

There is an important distinguishing characteristic of this miraculous speech. Those who spoke may have used their own language or just uttered sounds, however, those who heard or interpreted understood the words in their own languages.

As for Peter, it isn't made clear in Acts 2 whether he preached in tongues or not. However, since the text does say that they all spoke in tongues, it is highly probable that his message was in that miracle language. Saint Gregory the Theologian 329-389 believed that Peter spoke in a foreign language. Saint Gregory of Nyssa, a contemporary of St. Gregory the Theologian, taught that the speech was in Hebrew and the crowd heard in their own language the words that were spoken.[108]

Regardless of the verbal format of the message the result was a miracle. Acts 2:41 states, *"about three thousand were added to their number that day."* The significance of this miracle was the response, not the delivery.

3. Tongues should Edify not Confuse

Our God is not a spirit of disorder. He believes in order.

---

[108] Fr. Fred Bobosh, *On Pentecost, What Language was Heard,* orthochristian.com/ 104031.html., Blog -06/05/2017.

In fact, He commands it. 1 Corinthians 14:33 teaches us that, *"God is not a God of disorder but of peace--as in all the congregations of the Lord's people."* Anything that brings chaos to the congregation in worship is not of God.

There are many truths about speaking in tongues written in scripture. For instance, tongues must be spoken by one person at a time and be interpreted (1 Corinthians 14:27.) The word spoken must also edify the body (1 Corinthians 14:4). God's truth does not change since He doesn't change. *"Jesus is the same today, yesterday, and forever"* (Hebrews 13:8). The truth that applied in Paul's day is valid today.

4. Tongues will Cease:

It would be easy to echo most modern theological teaching that tongues vanished either at the time of the death of all of the Apostles or at the point of the canonization of Scripture. However, there is evidence of true speaking in tongues and interpretations of tongues among missionaries who are spreading the gospel message to previously undiscovered tribes.

Spiritual Application

Speaking in tongues has strong biblical support. Those who would seek this spiritual gift must follow God's rules. Since God remains the same, His laws also remain unchanged. Love is the key issue with all gifts of the Spirit. Love trumps all things and is the evidence of our salvation. "Love one another. As I have loved you, so you must love one another" (John 13:34). It's the law.

We know that speaking in tongues will cease. When Christ comes to take the church home, we will all speak a new tongue, the language of heaven.

Lessons within the Lesson

List and explain the original purpose of the gift for tongues.

What rules must be followed if someone seeks to speak in tongues?

When will tongues cease?

How do we reconcile tongues with God's love?

23. KNOWLEDGE WILL PASS AWAY

Prayer

Lord, God, we love your book the Bible. It contains Your words, only Your words, and the full revelation of Your thoughts. Your Word is Your truth for us. Help us to understand and apply what you have written to our lives that we might become Your obedient servants. In Christ's name, we pray, Amen!

Today's Scripture: 1 Corinthians 13:8d

Where there is knowledge it will pass away.

Associated Scriptures

For since the creation of the world His invisible attributes, His eternal power and divine nature, have been clearly seen, being understood through what has been made, so that they are without excuse (Romans 1:20.

The heavens are telling of the glory of God; And their expanse is declaring the work of His hands. Day to day pours forth speech, And night to night reveals knowledge. (Psalm 19:1-3).

and yet He did not leave Himself without witness, in that He did good and gave you rains from heaven and fruitful seasons, satisfying your hearts with food and gladness (Acts 14:17).

Correlative Quotes

There is no portion of it, even now, which may not be fitted, ...to furnish us valuable lessons.[109] – Albert Barnes

---

[109] Albert Barnes, *Notes Explanatory and Practical*, Public Domain, Ibid, P. 3993.

for reproof; of errors and heresies; this is the sword of the Spirit, which cuts all down.[110] – John Gill

For instruction…first he mentions instruction, which ranks above all the rest; (you can't) …exhort or reprove, if you have not previously instructed.[111] – John Calvin

For correction – For restoring things to their proper uses and places, correcting false notions and mistaken views.[112] – Adam Clarke

Author's Notes

INTRODUCTION

The introduction of this section of the verse introduces the third of three secondary gifts that the apostle says will go away; knowledge. Paul, through the inspiration of the Spirit of God, tells us in 1 Corinthians 13:8, *"that prophecies will cease, tongues will be stilled, and knowledge will pass away."*

The gift of knowledge does not refer to general knowledge. Anyone can know what the Bible teaches. The young child can explain Noah's Ark or Jonah and the giant fish. Adults with great knowledge of the scripture can recite verse upon verse exactly as it is written in or out of its context. Generally, knowledge simply means to know.

WHAT IS KNOWLEDGE?

Here is what we know about knowledge. Truth comes only from God. This Truth of God is delivered to us from the Holy Spirit who lives in believers. The Spirit of God has delivered God's Truth through the men and women He chose to write the Bible. The Bible tells us what has happened in the past, explains how we will survive the present, and what will happen to all mankind in the future. It is a completed book. The Bible is knowledge, God's knowledge.

---

[110] John Gill, *Commentary of the Whole Bible,* Public Domain, 1816, Ibid.

[111] John Calvin, *Commentaries on the Catholic Epistles*, Public Domain, Ibid, P. 202-203.

[112] Adam Clarke, *The Adam Clarke Commentary*, Public Domain, Ibid, P. 704.

As He inspired others to write God's book, The Spirit of God received a series of instructions from Jesus. He followed those commands. In John 14:26, Jesus teaches His disciples, *"But the Counselor, the Holy Spirit, whom the Father will send in my name, will teach you all things and will remind you of everything I have said to you."* Jesus repeats this thought in John 16:13 when He says, *"But when he, the Spirit of truth, comes, he will guide you into all the truth. He will not speak on his own; he will speak only what he hears, and he will tell you what is yet to come."*

ACKNOWLEDGMENT OF WHAT IS TO COME

"All Scripture is God-breathed and is useful for teaching, rebuking, correcting, and training in righteousness, so that the man of God may be thoroughly equipped for every good work" (2 Timothy 3:16-17).

This statement, in Timothy, refers to scriptural integrity or the sufficiency of Scripture. Scripture is an end in itself. No reputable, Spirit-led theologian believes in continuing revelation. The Scripture, the Holy Bible, is a completed document. It was completed by its final author, the apostle John, when he finished the Book of Revelation.

The Scripture is complete according to its own teaching. It contains all of the Truth of God for mankind. In Revelation 22:18-19, the final chapter of the final book written by God and recorded by the last living apostle states clearly and unequivocally, *"I warn everyone who hears the words of the prophecy of this scroll: If anyone adds anything to them, God will add to that person the plagues described in this scroll. And if anyone takes words away from this scroll of prophecy, God will take away from that person any share in the tree of life and in the Holy City, which are described in this scroll."*

HAS KNOWLEDGE PASSED AWAY?

The simple answer is no. We still have a living Word that can become deeper as we grow spiritually. The Spirit of God still interprets His Word according to our needs. When the gift of knowledge is used to help us understand God's Word and to help us adapt it to our lives that is a wise use of the Scriptures. If someone helps us to understand what God is saying in His word, that is also an acceptable use of the gift of knowledge. All knowledge that God transmits to us through His word whether it is directly or through another person is a Spiritual gift for which we should praise God. Anything shared with us other than a Scripture itself or scriptural interpretation should be ignored as another person's opinion. It is not the gift of knowledge.

Spiritual Application

God's knowledge is found in His Word, the Bible. His Word is the final word. When we read God's Word, His Spirit gives us understanding and wisdom. His wisdom allows us to apply His words to our lives. Hebrews 4:12 says, "*For the word of God is alive and active. Sharper than any double-edged sword, it penetrates even to dividing soul and spirit, joints and marrow; it judges the thoughts and attitudes of the heart.*" *If we need knowledge so that God can work in our lives to conform us to His image, Romans 8:29, we will find it in the "double-edged sword,*" Gods' Word.

Knowledge has not yet ceased. It lives in God's Word. When someone is given a word from God to help us through a difficult time or to send us in a new direction, it will be with scripture. Scripture is self-sufficient. His word will be instructional to our current and future situations in life. Not a human's word, but God's Word.

Lessons within the Lesson

Describe the gift of knowledge.

Explain the significance of the canonization of Scripture.

Give your own explanation of 2 Timothy 3:16-17.

Has the gift of knowledge passed away?

24. THAT WHICH IS COMPLETE

Prayer

We look for Your return Oh, Lord Jesus. We long for that day when You will come and take us home. The day when we will have the final victory over sin and death. At that time, You will rescue Your chosen children from the grips of suffering, the reward of the world, and bring us into everlasting peace. We pray for Your return, Amen!

Today's Scripture: 1 Corinthians 13:9-10

For we know in part and we prophesy in part, but when completeness comes, what is in part disappears.

Associated Scriptures

"In that day," declares the Lord, "you will call me 'my husband'; you will no longer call me 'my master'" (Hosea 2:16).

"Rejoice in that day and leap for joy, because great is your reward in heaven" (Luke 6:23).

"Shout and be glad, O Daughter of Zion. For I am coming, and I will live among you," declares the Lord. "Many nations will be joined with the Lord in that day and will become my people. I will live among you and you will know that the Lord Almighty has sent me to you (Zechariah 2:10-11).

Heaven and earth will pass away, but my words will never pass away (Matthew 24:35).

Correlative Quotes

When the great harvest-time comes, the instruments, however useful, will be cast aside altogether; the seeds will, by the very process of death, be transformed into blossoms and fruits, and in that perfected form remain forever.[113] – Charles John Ellicott

...the Spirit of God leads into all truth; the whole counsel of God is made known in the Scriptures, and by the ministers of the word, ...and every truth of the Gospel is known...[114] – John Gill

Human knowledge, at best but the spellings of babes, will vanish in the perfect light of heaven. Eloquence will seem like the lisping of infancy. Prophecies will have no place, because all the landscape of the future will be revealed.[115] – F. B. Meyer

Author's Notes

INTRODUCTION

Christianity is an intellectual religion as distinct from religions of ritual and ceremony. ...It is well that the infirmity and imperfection of our knowledge should be brought vividly before our minds, as it is in this passage. At the same time, provision is made against discouragement by an assurance that the partial and transitory shall be succeeded by the perfect and the eternal.[116] – Spence and Excell

We have now reached a significant turning point in the text of this chapter. We are about to move from the earthly impact of love to its eternal importance. As we look at the interpretation of these two strategic verses, we see a picture of man's current understanding and interpretation of the Truth of God as it relates to love, followed by that which will be absolute. God's Truth is complete and concrete (John 17:17).

---

[113] C. J. Ellicott, (Charles John), *A New Testament Commentary for English Readers*, Vol. 2, 1897. Public Domain, Ibid, P. 339.

[114] John Gill, *John Gill's Exposition of the Entire Bible*, 1810, Public Domain, Ibid P. 306.

[115] Fredrick Brotherton Meyer, Our Daily Homily, Public Domain, 1899, Ibid, P. 146.

[116] H. D. M. Spence and Joseph S. Exell, *The Pulpit Commentary*, Public Domain, Ibid, P.446.

1. <u>We Perceive in Part</u>: 1 Corinthians 13:9a, *"For we know in part."*

      The incomplete nature of the Truth of God as assembled and formulated in the mind of man is temporal. God's Truth is eternal. We only have to read a few commentaries on these particular verses to see that mankind does not agree on Gods' perfect intent. This applies to all of scripture. God's Truth as presented by the Holy Spirit and written by men is accurate in every way but interpreted in many ways based on the bias of those who make such decisions. No one person has the full revelation of God's word.

2. <u>Partial Prophesy</u>: 1 Corinthians 13:9b, *"we prophesy in part."*

      As we look at prophecy through the microscope of scripture, we realize that it too is incomplete. We can learn enough to secure a glimpse of eternity but not enough to determine the whole picture. In Daniel 12:8 the vision causes him to ask, *"I heard, but I did not understand. So, I asked, "My lord, what will the outcome of all this be?" He replied, "Go your way, Daniel, because the words are rolled up and sealed until the time of the end."*

      In Mark 13:31-32, Jesus says, *"Heaven and earth will pass away, but my words will never pass away. But about that day or hour, no one knows, not even the angels in heaven, nor the Son, but only the Father."*

3. <u>The Perfect is Coming</u>: 1 Corinthians 13:10a, *"but when completeness comes"*

      God's Truth will not cease to be the truth. We will actually experience the whole Truth of God as it unfolds at the end. The visions of the Book of Revelation will become a reality to all believers and unbelievers.

4. <u>The Partial Disappears</u>: 1 Corinthians 13:10b, *"what is in part disappears"*

      In the last days the universe will pass away and there will be a new heaven and new earth will be created (Isaiah 66:21-23, Isaiah 65:17-18, 2 Peter 3:12-14, and Revelation 21:1-8). The glorious redemption of mankind and all of creation will come to a crescendo followed by the final act of justification. That which was predicted will be fulfilled.

We do not see the full picture now. As humans, with our frailties and fallibility, we can only imagine what our minds can understand. Since we cannot comprehend that which is beyond the scope and measure of our limited ability to dream, we are unable to anticipate the spectacular.

> Our prospect is not one to inspire melancholy; or if a shade of pensiveness pass over the soul in the prospect of the disappearance of what is so familiar and so dear, that pensiveness may well give way to content and hope when we look forward to the glory which shall be revealed.[117] – Spence and Excell

Spiritual Application

As Scripture tells us, we are to study God's Word to be obedient to Him (2 Timothy 2:15) and to grow spiritually (2 Peter 3:18). The Word is perfect. It is a function of the Holy Spirit given to writers who God trusted. However, its interpretation can sometimes be imperfect since it lacks a full understanding of God's intent. As we study, the Spirit of God brings the Word into a clearer focus so that it can adequately transform our thinking and our lives. That is the intent of the whole of Scripture.

Lessons within the Lesson

In the movie A Few Good Men, Colonel Jessup when asked to give the court the truth utters the famous line, "You can't handle the truth." How does this statement pertain to the bible quote in 1 Corinthians 13:9, "*For we know in part and prophesy in part.*"

Why will God's Truth not cease to be the truth?

What will happen to the current Truth as we see it in the Bible?

How do we apply 1 Corinthians 13:9-10 to our lives today?

---

[117] H. D. M. Spence and Joseph S. Exell, *The Pulpit Commentary*, Public Domain, Ibid, P.446.

25. LOVE PUTS AWAY CHILDISH THINGS

Prayer

Oh, Lord, our God, and Savior, we ask You this day to convict us to walk in Your light and be led by Your Spirit. We desire to serve You and You alone. Our lives are an open vessel ready to be filled with Your Love. Lead us by Your Spirit this day and every day, in Jesus name we pray, Amen!

Today's Scripture: 1 Corinthians 13:11

When I was a child, I talked like a child, I thought like a child, I reasoned like a child. When I became a man, I put the ways of childhood behind me.

Associated Scriptures

but speaking the truth in love, we are to grow up in all aspects into Him who is the head, even Christ (Ephesians 4:15)

Therefore, leaving the elementary teaching about the *Christ, let us press on to maturity, not laying again a foundation of repentance from dead works and of faith toward God* (Hebrews 6:10).

...like newborn babies, long for the pure milk of the word, so that by it you may grow in respect to salvation (1 Peter 2:2).

Correlative Quotes

What narrow views, what confused and indistinct notions of things, have children, in comparison of grown men! And how naturally do men, when reason is ripened and matured, despise and relinquish their infant thoughts, put them away, reject them, esteem as nothing![118] – Matthew Henry

There are many things that are suitable to children, which are afterwards done away on arriving at maturity.[119] – John Calvin

when we became men-adults, having gained much knowledge of men and things, we spoke and reasoned more correctly, having left off all the manners and habits of our childhood.[120] – Adam Clarke

Author's Notes

INTRODUCTION

Generally speaking, when children begin to talk, their first word is usually either "mama" or "dada" (depending on who has been whispering in their ear the most). The next word is usually "no". According to psychologists, this reaction results from hearing the word "no" continuously. The next most common word is "MINE." This word is generally accompanied by a strongly possessive attitude. Surprisingly, this is not a word that they have heard frequently unless they have an older sibling.

The Corinthians acted and reacted as spoiled spiritual children. They learned the words "no" and "mine" long ago. One would think that with their new loving hearts, they would have been opened to sharing even if they didn't learn it as children. We would be wrong.

1. A Blessed Church: 1 Corinthians 1:7, "*Therefore you do not lack any spiritual gift as you eagerly wait for our Lord Jesus Christ to be revealed.*"

The Corinthian church had been established by Paul on a firm foundation. They had been saved by the grace of Jesus (vv. 4-

---

[118] Matthew Henry, *Matthew Henry Concise Commentary on the Whole Bible (Unabridged), Volume VI, Acts to Revelation*, Public Domain, 1706, Ibid. P. 821.

[119] John Calvin, *Commentaries on the Catholic Epistles*, Rights: Public Domain, Ibid. , P. 266.

[120] Adam Clarke, *The Adam Clarke Commentary Corinthians through Philemon*, Public Domain, 1836, Ibid, P. 144

5). In addition, they had been blessed to hear messages presented with the eloquence of speech and had received an understanding of the mysteries of Scripture as was the testimony of others (vs.1:5). As a result, the Corinthians had willingly accepted the gift of salvation (vs. 1:6).

To meet the many spiritual needs of their sizable flock, God had given everyone in the congregation spiritual gifts to help them (vs. 1:7). Finally, God had richly blessed the Corinthian church. Since the congregation had many rich members, they should have had plenty for everyone to enjoy.

2. A Church in Turmoil: 1 Corinthians 1:10-31.

At the time of this first letter to the Corinthian church, there was great turmoil. Infighting was causing division. Pride had reared its ugly head and the members of this community had succumbed to it. In addition, their pride had produced disunity (vv. 10-11).

Their main issue of pride concerned how each one had been led to a saving knowledge of Jesus. The Corinthians were boasting about the origin of their salvation (vv. 1:12). Some were bragging that Paul himself had led them to Christ. Others traced their salvation back to Apollos, some to Cephas, and the balance credited Christ. Paul's response is simple but profound, *"Is Christ divided? Was Paul crucified for you? Were you baptized in the name of Paul"* (1:13)?

Paul followed with answers to these rhetorical questions. In 1 Corinthians 1:18-30. He writes in part (vs. 18), *"For the message of the cross is foolishness to those who are perishing, but to us who are being saved it is the power of God."* Then Paul finishes this section of scripture with this important truth (vv. 30-31), *"It is because of him that you are in Christ Jesus, who has become for us wisdom from God--that is, our righteousness, holiness, and redemption. Therefore, as it is written: "Let the one who boasts boast in the Lord."*

3. A Church with Issues:

In addition to the arguing over the origins of their

conversion, the disunity of its members caused several other devastating issues within the Corinthians' church.

The root cause of their slide into unrighteousness was their worldliness. They had assented to its temptations and positioned the things of this world ahead of God. They had become an immoral church. They were practicing sexual sin (5:1) and drunkenness (11:21). Paul called them the carnal church in 3:1-3. Finally, they were a dysfunctional church (11:17-22).

Spiritual Application

In Matthew 12:28, Jesus tells us that a house divided against itself cannot stand. A house divided phrase clearly applies to the Corinthian church. They were blessed by God with a solid foundation of teaching by the apostle Paul. In addition, they were given every gift of the Spirit to supply the power to interpret the message of God for personal spiritual growth. This power was also to be used to reach others for Jesus and to disciple those who were converted.

In spite of all that God accomplished through Paul and the gospel message, the Corinthians' pride and arrogance caused them to put themselves ahead of Christ forcing Him to be secondary in importance to the world and its sin. As a result of these spiritual failures, pride crept into the equation. When we are filled with pride there is no room for love.

Lessons within the Lesson

What was the greatest strength of the Corinthians? Read 1 Corinthians 1:1-9.

What was their greatest weakness?

How did Paul address these weaknesses? Read 1 Corinthians 1:10-31

Explain how we can avoid the error of the Corinthians church.

26. LOVE WILL HELP US SEE JESUS

Prayer:

My ears had heard of You but now my eyes have seen You. Therefore, I despise myself and repent in dust and ashes (Job 42:5-6). Oh, Lord Jesus, we seek Your face as Job. However, we want others to see You reflected in our lives every moment of every day. Lead us, Lord, in Christ's name we pray, Amen!

Today's Scripture: 1 Corinthians 13:12a

For now, we see only a reflection as in a mirror; then we shall see face to face.

Associated Scriptures

The precepts of the Lord are right, giving joy to the heart. The commands of the Lord are radiant, giving light to the eyes (Psalms 19:8).

My eyes are ever on the Lord, for only he will release my feet from the snare (Psalms 25:15).

lift up my eyes to you, to you whose throne is in heaven (Psalms 123:1).

Correlative Quotes

Now we see - Even the things that surround us. But by means of a glass - Or mirror, which reflects only their imperfect forms, in a dim, faint, obscure manner; so that our thoughts about them are puzzling and intricate, and everything is a kind of riddle to us. But then - We shall see, not a faint reflection, but the objects themselves. Face to face - Distinctly.[121] – John Wesley

---

[121] John Wesley, *John Wesley's Notes of the Bible*, Public Domain, Publication date 1755, Ibid, P. 321.

The reflection seeming to the eye to be behind the mirror, so that we see it through the mirror. Ancient mirrors were made of polished brass or other metals. The contrast is between the inadequate knowledge of an object gained by seeing it reflected in a dim mirror (such as ancient mirrors were), compared with the perfect idea we have of it by seeing itself directly.[122] – Jamieson, Fausset, Brown

If we remember the imperfect metal surfaces which formed the mirrors of those days, we can imagine how imperfect and enigmatical the (Greek word is in an "enigma" would the image appear.[123] – C. J. Ellicott

Author's Notes

Introduction

It is pleasant to talk about this, but what will we see when the pearl gates open? The streets of gold will have small attraction to us, and the harps of angels will but slightly enchant us, compared with the King in the midst of the throne. He it is who shall rivet our gaze, absorb our thoughts, enchain our affection, and move all our sacred passions to their highest pitch of celestial ardor. We shall see Jesus.[124] – Charles Spurgeon

The image that one would see in a mirror, even the best mirrors, at the time of the apostles would be indistinct (HCSB). The reflection would most probably be, at best, like "puzzling reflections" (NLT), "blurred" (GWT) or obscured (CJB). The world system with its deep hatred for a one God theology provided the ideal object for Paul to use in describing the way we would see Jesus in the future.

---

[122] Jamieson, Robert, D. D.; Fausset, A. R.; Brown, David, *Commentary Critical and Explanatory on the Whole Bible*, Public Domain 1871, Copy Freely, Ibid, P. 3562

[123] C. J. Ellicott, (Charles John), *A New Testament Commentary for English Readers*, Vol. 2, 1897. Public Domain, 1897, Ibid, P. 339.

[124] Charles Spurgeon, *Now and Then*, Public Domain, Sermon #1002, spurgeongems.org/vols16-18/chs1002.pdf, P. 5

Paul saw Jesus. Jesus appeared to Him, in the flesh, on the road to Damascus. He was not looking at the Son of God in a mirror dimly (ESV) or darkly (KJV). He saw Jesus in the flesh. This was not a perverted reflection, but the real Jesus. Paul saw the glorified Christ. He saw the light of the world; an eminence brighter than all the light found in the universe. Paul immediately went blind (Acts 9:8). After three days of blindness, Jesus removed the protective film that covered Paul's eyes so that he could once again see (Acts 9:18).

The mirror was not an object that Paul needed. Instead, the obscure reflection was an expression of how others who have not seen the resurrected and glorified Christ would see him. We see Jesus by faith and not by sight. Believers today witness the dim reflection of Jesus through the Word (John 1:14). The true light will only be seen in the life to come. Now we see a reflection. We see it in our fellow Christians (1 John 2:8). Finally, we see it in the miracles that Jesus still accomplishes here on earth (John 14:12).

JESUS REFLECTED IN THE WORD

John 1:14, "*The Word became flesh and made his dwelling among us. We have seen his glory, the glory of the one and only Son, who came from the Father, full of grace and truth.*"

We must accept Jesus by faith. John and the other apostles were fortunate that they, from the beginning of Christ's ministry, were able to hear him speak. They could see him with their own eyes. They touched him with their hands. This personal contact they proclaimed through the Word of Life (1 John 1:1-2). We have the amazing documentation of those who did witness the life, the love, and the miracle that was the Son of God.

JESUS REFLECTED IN US

1 John 2:8, "*Yet I am writing you a new command; its truth is seen in him and in you because the darkness is passing and the true light is already shining.*"

Everything we say or do directly reflects on the One who is the center of the universe (Psalm 19:1-5). The One who keeps all things in order according to His will (Psalm 147:15). Jesus rescued us to be His light to the world. When Jesus returns, He will free us from this temporary housing. It its place, we will receive a permanent residence that is without sin or decay. Our new bodies will be indestructible and without flaw (2 Corinthians 5:10. We shall be made perfect in Jesus.

JESUS REFLECTED IN MIRACLES

John 14:12, "*Truly I tell you, the one who believes in me will also do the works that I do. And he will do even greater works than these, because I am going to the Father.*"

The miracles of Jesus were undeniable pieces of the evidence of His existence. He healed the blind and made the lame walk. He cleansed the leper and brought the dead back to life (Matthew 11:5). He overcame Satan's temptation on three separate occasions (Matthew 4:1-11). Jesus fed the five thousand (Matthew 14:13-21). Only God could do these things. He was the physical representation of God the father.

More than five hundred witnesses saw Jesus after He raised himself from the dead (1 Corinthians 15:6). We will surely see Him again as Jesus predicted.

Spiritual Application

Now we see Jesus through His Spirit that lives in us. We see Him in the testimony of the disciples and others who actually lived with Jesus. Our personal witness will come later when we see Him come in the clouds. He will return as the almighty, all powerful, all knowing God of creation. Now we see in a mirror darkly. But then, we will see Jesus face to face.

Lessons within the Lesson

Why is the image that Paul spoke of dim or distorted?

What does, "the Word became flesh and dwelt among us" mean?

In what way did God fulfill his promises to mankind?

What miracle(s) have you seen in your lifetime that could only have been from Jesus?

27. WE WILL KNOW FULLY

Prayer

Our relationship is built and sustained by faith in You Oh, Lord. You are not only the foundation and mainstay of our faith. You are its object. You are our hope of survival on this earth and our guarantee of life eternal. We praise You, Lord! We worship Your name above every name, Amen!

Today's Scripture: 1 Corinthians 13:12b

Now I know in part; then I shall know fully, even as I am fully known.

Associated Scriptures

God said to Solomon, "Since this is your heart's desire and you have not asked for wealth, riches or honor, nor for the death of your enemies, and since you have not asked for a long life but for wisdom and knowledge to govern my people over whom I have made you king, 12 therefore wisdom and knowledge will be given you (2 Chronicles 1:11-12).

Do you know how the clouds are balanced, those wondrous works of Him who is perfect in knowledge (Job 37:16, NKJV)?

Teach me good judgment and knowledge, for I believe Your commandments (Psalms 119:66, NKJV).

The fear of the Lord is the beginning of knowledge, But fools despise wisdom and instruction (Proverbs 1:7, KNJV).

Correlative Quotes

How vast the disparity between the speech, understanding, and reasoning of Saul, the little Jewish boy, and "Paul, the aged," the great theologian and sublime apostle! This is only a faint type of the difference between the Christian here and the Christian yonder.[125] – H.D.M. Spence and Joseph Exell

Now we can only discern things at a great distance, as through a telescope, and that involved in clouds and obscurity; but hereafter the things to be known will be near and obvious, open to our eyes; and our knowledge will be free from all obscurity and error. God is to be seen face to face; and we are to know him as we are known by him; not indeed as perfectly, but in some sense in the same manner.[126] – Matthew Henry

Like that image which you see when you look at an object in a mirror far off. with blurred and undefined outline, such is our knowledge here and now; but then (i.e., when this dispensation is at an end we shall see as you see a man when you stand before him face to face.[127] – Charles John Ellicott

Author's Notes

INTRODUCTION

And how much more shall we understand when raised to that higher sphere and endowed with brighter faculties, none of us can tell.[128] – Charles Spurgeon

No one person has the complete revelation of God. No one person, other than Jesus, has ever known everything about God or even had a clear understanding of His Word and its purpose for mankind. There have been hundreds, maybe thousands, of complete commentaries written to explain God's Word. As we study

---

[125] H. D. M. Spence and Joseph S. Exell, *The Pulpit Commentary*, Public Domain, Ibid, P. 170.

[126] Matthew Henry, *Matthew Henry Concise Commentary on the Whole Bible (Unabridged), Volume IV*, Public Domain, 1706, Ibid, P. 821

[127] C. J. Ellicott, (Charles John), *A New Testament Commentary for English Readers*, Vol. 2, 1897. Public Domain, 1897, Ibid,

[128] Charles Spurgeon, *Now, and Then*, Public Domain, Public Domain, Ibid, P. 4.

these works of mankind, we see that they are not always in agreement with each other. Even though many of the authors thought that they had complete knowledge and understanding of the Scripture, they didn't.

> I have fancied sometimes that the elucidations (explanations) of learned doctors of divinity if they could be submitted to the very least in the kingdom of heaven, would only cause them to smile at the learned ignorance of the sons of earth.[129] – Charles Spurgeon

It is only when reaching Heaven that we will truly know God's completed plan, purpose, and the promises that He had designed specifically for us. Then we will see ourselves as God sees us. Only then will we receive the instantaneous discernment and spontaneous perspective of spiritual truth.

1. "*Now I Know in Part*";

> There are some grand doctrines, brothers and sisters, we dearly love, but though we love them, our understanding is too feeble to grasp them fully. We account them to be mysteries; we reverently acknowledge them, yet we dare not attempt to explain them; they are matters of faith to us.[130] – Charles Spurgeon

The Bible is the Truth of God. It is God's word (John 1:1). Through salvation and by the teaching of the Spirit of God we continually grow in the knowledge of the Truth (John 14:26). As we understand His Word, we apply it to our lives. We call this transitional operation of the Spirit transformation. As we are being transformed, God is able to use us to move His plan and purpose forward. Romans 12:1 confirms this Truth. "*...be transformed by the renewing of your mind. Then you will be able to test and approve what God's will is--his good, pleasing and perfect will.*"

---

[129] Charles Spurgeon, Ibid.

[130] Charles Spurgeon, Ibid.

2. "*Then I Shall Know Fully*":

> Probably things that puzzle us here will be as plain as possible there; we shall perhaps smile at our own ignorance. Oh, how little we know, but how much we shall know![131] – Charles Spurgeon

Now we only know in part. As a result, we can only learn, teach, or even preach in part. That which is perfect, Christ, has not yet returned to meet us face to face. It is at this point that we will know fully. It is at this moment in time that we will put away the childish arguments and put on the wisdom of men, God's wisdom.

Since we know in part, we can only interpret in part. Incomplete knowledge and understanding of Scripture cause debate leading to disputes as mankind tries to make sense of God's hidden mysteries. A good example of a controversial verse is found in John 3:5, "Jesus answered, "*Truly, truly, I say to you, unless one is born of water and the Spirit, he cannot enter the kingdom of God.*"

Interpretation #1: Adam Clarke states that the water and the Spirit are the same thing and therefore the statement is considered to be redundant in meaning or "an elliptical form of speech" with the words "water" and "spirit" having the same meaning.[132]

Interpretation #2: John Wesley considered the water to be secondary in importance to the Spirit. The Spirit becomes part of us in rebirth and the water refers to water baptism which follows spiritual rebirth. Wesley says, "and be baptized (wherever baptism can be had) as the outward sign and means of it (it referring to the indwelling of the Spirit, author's note)."[133]

---

[131] Charles Spurgeon, Now, and Then, Public Domain, Ibid. P. 5

[132] Adam Clarke, *The Adam Clarke Commentary, John to Romans*, Public Domain, 1836, Thomas Tegg and Son, 73 Cheapside, London. godrules.net/library/clarke/clarkegen 1.htm, P. 43.

[133] John Wesley, *John Wesley's Notes of the Bible*, Public Domain, 1755, Ibid, P. 150.

Interpretation #3: Albert Barnes taught that the water referred to water baptism, "The water here is evidently signified baptism." He continues to show how it precedes spiritual rebirth and is essential for new birth and church membership."[134]   Barnes believed that either baptism of water and of Spirit are one and the same and cannot be separated.   This spiritualizes the word water.

Interpretation #4: A. T. Robertson suggests, "Some insist on the language in verse 6 as meaning the birth of the flesh coming in a sack of water in contrast to the birth of the Spirit."[135]   In this interpretation, the water, when released, is a sign preceding physical birth. This belief, of physical birth, makes sense in the context of Nicodemus' question and following response in verse four.   It also coincides with the response of Jesus in verse 6, "Flesh gives birth to flesh but the Spirit gives birth to Spirit."

This is only one example of the confusion that come with not "knowing fully." Once our time on earth has ended and we are fully resurrected with Christ as His bride we shall "know fully."

3. "*Even as I am Fully Known*":

We shall know even as we are known. Besides, dear friends, the atmosphere of heaven is so much clearer than this, that I do not wonder we can see better there; here is the smoke of daily care; the constant dust of toil; the fog of trouble perpetually rising. We cannot be expected to see much in such a smoky atmosphere as this. But when we shall pass beyond, we shall find no clouds ever gather round the sun to hide its everlasting brightness. There all is clear; the daylight is serene as the noonday; we shall be in a clearer atmosphere and brighter light.[136] – Charles Spurgeon

---

[134] Albert Barnes, *Notes Explanatory and Practical*, Public Domain, 1845, Ibid, P. 1070

[135] A. T. Robertson, *New Testament Word Pictures Volume 6*, Public Domain. Copy Freely, Ibid, P. 652.

[136] Charles Spurgeon, Now, and Then, Public Domain, Ibid. P. 6

Now I know in part – Even when God himself reveals things to me, great part of them is still kept under the veil. But then I shall know even as also I am known - In a clear, full, comprehensive manner; in some measure like God, who penetrates the center of every object, and sees at one glance through my soul and all things.[137] – John Wesley

When we see Jesus "face to face" in all His amazing glory, we will know as we are known by God (1 Thessalonians 4:13-18). Now we have a partial view of Heaven, Jesus, God, and His Spirit. Then we shall see them "face to face." We will never be omniscient; however, we will know all that we should know about ourselves, others, and the Trinity that will rule and reign over us forever and ever. How sweet will be the knowledge received. How wonderous will be the place where we live. How enlightening will be our relationship with the creators.

Spiritual Application

Today we can know, understand, and apply most of what we are taught in Scripture. However, even the most knowledgeable biblical scholars cannot know everything. Those mysteries of scripture have been hidden from us for our own good. When the resurrection comes, the mysteries of scripture will be opened and we will say, "WOW, so that's how it all fits together." We will never know everything. Only the Trinity is omniscient. Some things will remain hidden from us.

Lessons within the Lesson

What do we now only know in part?

Why do we only know it in part now?

What action of God will allow us to understand what we will know fully? Read 1 Thessalonians 4:13-18.

What does John mean when he says, "Even as I am known?"

---

[137] John Wesley, *John Wesley's Notes of the Bible*, Public Domain, Publication date 1755, Ibid, P. 321.

28. FAITH, HOPE, LOVE REMAIN

Prayer

Our Lord, and our God, please continue to give us the faith to make the many decisions in life. Give us the hope that will allow us to function in the maze we call the world. Give us the wisdom to utilize faith and hope as You have designed them. In Christ's name, Amen!

Today's Scripture: 1 Corinthians 13:13

And now these three remain: faith, hope, and love.

Associated Scriptures

So, faith comes from hearing, and hearing through the word of Christ (Romans 10:17, ESV).

For whatever was written in former days was written for our instruction, that through endurance and through the encouragement of the Scriptures we might have hope (Romans 15:4, ESV).

Let all that you do be done in love (1 Corinthians 16:4, ESV).

Correlative Quotes

ABIDE; namely, after the extraordinary gifts have ceased; for those three are necessary and sufficient for salvation at all times, whereas the extraordinary gifts are not at all so.[138] – Jamieson, Fausset, Brown

Faith, by which we apprehend spiritual blessings, and walk with God. Hope, by which we view and expect eternal blessedness, and pass through things temporal so as not to lose those which are eternal. Charity or love, by which we show forth the virtues of the grace

---

[138] Jamieson, Robert, D. D.; Fausset, A. R.; Brown, David, *Commentary Critical and Explanatory on the Whole Bible*, Public Domain, 1871, Copy Freely, Ibid, P. 3563.

which we receive by faith in living a life of obedience to God, and of good will and usefulness to man.[139] – Adam Clarke

The word means, properly, to remain, continue, abide; and is applied to persons remaining in a place, in a state or condition, in contradistinction from removing or changing their place, or passing away. Here it must be understood to be used to denote permanency, when the other things of which he had spoken had passed away; and the sense is, that faith, hope, and love would remain...[140] – Albert Barnes

Author's Notes

INTRODUCTION

Faith, hope, and love are the key ingredients in our connection with God, His Son Jesus, and the Holy Spirit that lives in us. Faith is the gift that saves, justifies, and maintains the believer's relationship with God (Ephesians 2:8-9). Hope is the gift of God that lays a foundation for future growth in Christ and anchors the vision of our future with Him (Jeremiah 29:11). Love is the evidence of our relationship with God (1 John 2:4-5).

FAITH

Habakkuk 2:4 teaches *"Look, his ego is inflated; he is without integrity. But the righteous one will live by his faith."* The proud are filled with themselves. They don't need or do they request any help. They know the way and they want all the credit. This is a picture of the majority of humanity. They would not ask another person to help them with anything. Most of all they would not believe or trust in God. That would mean they must give away the credit.

The proud are more than willing to assume the responsibility

[139] Adam Clarke, *The New Testament of our Lord and Savior Jesus Christ, A Commentary and Critical Notes, Romans to Revelation*, Ibid, P. 146-147.

[140] Albert Barnes, *Notes Explanatory and Practical*, Public Domain, Ibid, P. 2736.

as long as they are going to receive the credit. When they have completed a task, they blatantly shout their success to anyone who will listen and also to those who would rather not.

However, the righteous, those who are justified by faith, are not interested in receiving any credit. They understand that every good and perfect gift comes from God (James 1:17). The just recognize that they have become the instruments used by God to accomplish His work, His desires. The righteous believe that God works in us and through us to perform His will here on earth (Philippians 2:13). We are His tools.

HOPE

> Rejoice in hope, be patient in tribulation, be constant in prayer (Romans 12:12, ESV).

God never intended for us to experience stress, grief, anguish, and suffering. His plan was for us to live forever, in paradise, serving and worshiping Him. It was through our own disobedience that we brought suffering upon ourselves. Romans 3:23 explains, *"For all have sinned and come short of the glory of God."*

But Here we are in today's world, some face problems so deep and devastating that they suffer from daily depression. We have problems at home, with our offspring, in our marriages, and yes even in our churches.

People place their hope in earthly things and people instead of an eternal God. Just as there is no salvation outside of faith in Jesus Christ, there is no hope outside of an ongoing relationship with God. Romans 5:1-2 tells us, *"Therefore, having been justified by faith, we have peace with God through our Lord Jesus Christ, through whom also we have access by faith into this grace in which we stand, and rejoice in **HOPE** of the glory of God."* Like faith, hope is a gift from God

How do we develop HOPE on a daily basis? Just as faith ignites and renews our relationship with God daily, HOPE gives us the inner strength and assurance to prepare ourselves for the future.

LOVE

...everyone derives advantage from his own faith and hope, but love extends its benefits to others.[141] – John Calvin

Love is special. Love transforms us into the image of God. The easiest thing in the world to say is, "I love you." The most difficult thing in the world is living it.

God's Love is sacrificial (Ephesians 5:2). His love sent Jesus to the cross. His love is also personal (John 21:15-17). He offers us eternal life for free. God's Love is unchangeable (Hebrews 13:8). God Is immutable. He does not change. Finally, God's love is eternal. In Jeremiah 31:3 God says, "*I have loved you with an everlasting love; I have drawn you with unfailing kindness.*"

Spiritual Application

Faith as defined by Hebrews 11:1 (ESV) is "*Now faith is the assurance of things hoped for, the conviction of things not seen.* Hope on the other hand is means a strong belief about things in the future. Romans 8:25 (CSB) says, "*we hope for what we do not see*"

Faith and hope are not characteristics of God. If God had to trust, He wouldn't be God. If God had to hope or believe, He would not be omniscient. Faith and hope as we see them in the Bible are temporal. Love, on the other hand, is a characteristic of God. God is Love (1 John 4:8). He loves because He is the God of love. Love is superior because it is the essence of faith and hope. It is love that allows us to have faith and hope.

Lessons within the Lesson

What is faith? How do we express faith in our lives?

What is hope? How do we express hope in our lives?

Why is love special? How do we express love in our lives?

---

[141] John Calvin, Ibid, P. 268.

---

29. THE ETERNAL NATURE OF LOVE

Prayer

Praise the Lord , O my soul; all my inmost being, praise his holy name. Praise the Lord , O my soul, and forget not all his benefits – who forgives all your sins and heals all your diseases, who redeems your life from the pit and crowns you with love and compassion...(Psalms 103:1-4). Praise God with the highest praise and give Him glory through all the ages, Amen!

Today's Scripture: 1 Corinthians 13:13b

But the greatest of these is love.

Associated Scriptures

Love is eternal (1 Corinthians 13:8).

For God so loved the world that he gave his one and only Son, that whoever believes in him shall not perish but have eternal life (John 3:16).

See what great love the Father has lavished on us, that we should be called children of God! (1 John 3:1).

Correlative Quotes

...he that has true faith in Christ, shall die in it; and he that has a good hope through grace, shall have it in his death; and love will outlive death, and be in its height and glory in the other world.[142] – John Gill

Love is properly the image of God in the soul; for God is LOVE.[143] – Adam Clarke

Most commentators have supposed that Paul is

---

[142] John Gill, *Commentary of the Whole Bible*, Public Domain, 1816, Ibid, P. 311.
[143] Adam Clarke, Ibid, P. 147.

speaking here only of this life, and that he means to say that in this life these three exist; that "faith, hope, and charity exist in this scene "only," but that in the future world faith and hope will be done away, and therefore the greatest of these is charity"[144] – Albert Barnes

Author's Notes

INTRODUCTION

Anyone who does not love does not know God, because God is love (1 John 4:8, ESV).

Faith, hope, love - Are the sum of perfection on earth; love alone is the sum of perfection in heaven.[145] – John Wesley

Even when love is a noun, it's a verb. It is an action of the will, fostered by the Spirit of God (1 Corinthians 13:4-8). "Love isn't something that we're in, it's something that we do." - Clint Black

LOVE ETERNAL

The word "faith" occurs 270 times in the Bible. Hope appears 166 times. The word "love" is written 551 times in the Bible. The phrases *"God's love," "Love of God,"* and *"His love"* appear 68 times in the Bible. In Psalm 139 the phrase "His love endures forever," is repeated 26 times in its 26 verses. Love is a very important issue with God.

The phrase *"But the greatest of these is love,"* as found in 1 Corinthians 13:13 indicates that love is more important than either faith or hope. It is faith that rescues us from eternal damnation (Luke 7:50). Hope continually gives us assurance of our position with God (Hebrews 6:19). Both faith and hope are extremely important biblical and spiritual truths with eternal consequences to the believer. They are essential to the whole plan for salvation and spiritual growth. However, both faith and hope are functions of God's love.

---

[144] Albert Barnes, *Notes Explanatory and Practical*, Public Domain, Ibid.

> *But because of his great **love** for us, God, who is rich in **mercy**, made us alive with Christ even when we were dead in transgressions – it is by **grace** you have been saved* (Ephesians 2:4-5).

> *For it is by **grace** you have been saved, through **faith** – and this not from yourselves, it is the gift of God – no by works, so that no one can boast* (Ephesians 2:8-9).

As we consider love, we cannot ignore mercy, grace, faith, and hope.

1. Mercy:

Mercy is an expression of the love of God. It occurs when we don't get what we do deserve. Because it is our nature to be disobedient, we break God's most important commandments; love God, love all others. As a result of our bad behavior, we all deserve eternal punishment and separation from God. However, in His mercy, God does not give us what we have earned. Instead of administering His justice for our unbelief and subsequent disobedience, He offers us the gift of eternal life.

2. Grace:

Grace is like mercy. It is the opposite in its definition while accomplishing the same results. Grace is when we do get what we don't deserve. We don't deserve eternal life. We can't earn eternal life since we are naturally evil (Romans 3:23). Through grace, by faith, we receive salvation as a free gift. Grace is an expression of God's love. Grace produces faith. Faith ignites redemption. Redemption causes justification (Romans 5:1).

The gift of eternal life occurs as a result of God's grace. James 1:17 emphasizes this fact when it says, *"Every good and perfect gift is from above, coming down from the Father of the heavenly lights, who does not change like shifting shadows."* All

---

[145] John Wesley, Ibid, P. 321.

---

that we have or ever will have is a gift from God and a result of His grace. The gifts that God gives us are too numerous to describe. God continually showers His grace upon us. The apostle Paul describes this phenomenon when he writes, *"The grace of our Lord was poured out on me abundantly, along with the faith and love that are in Christ Jesus"* (1Timothy 1:14).

3. Faith:

Faith is another bi-product of love. Hebrews 11:1 defines faith when it explains, *"Now faith is the assurance of things hoped for, the conviction of things not seen."* This verse in Hebrews sets forth the doctrine of faith. Faith is the action of God's grace in mankind that establishes and seals the gift of salvation. First, It gives us God's pledge and guarantees that we will have eternal life with Him through Christ. Secondly, Faith gives us the confidence that we are anchored to those future blessings which He has planned for us here on earth along with the eternal things that we cannot see.

4. Hope:

There is no action of mankind that warrants salvation; none (Romans 3:10). There is nothing mankind can do to earn eternal life, nothing. The unconditional love of God remains the only option for forgiveness. Our only alternative is the hope we find in the sacrifice and resurrection of Jesus.

Spiritual Application

The greatest of these is love. The love of God is the source of mercy, grace, faith, and hope. Romans 6:23 says, *"For the wages of sin is death, but the gift of God is eternal life through Jesus Christ our Lord."*

Lessons within the Lesson

Explain the difference between mercy and grace.

How are both mercy and grace the same?

How does faith ignite salvation?

What will God's gift of hope accomplish for Christians?

30. GOD'S LOVE: NEVER FAILS

Prayer

Oh Lord, my Lord, how majestic is your name in all the earth (Psalm 8:9). Your love has freed us from the hands of the enemy. It is the hope that secures us for the future. It is by Your hand that You have sheltered us from the temptations of this world. Thank You, Oh, God, for Your sustaining power and presence. In and through Jesus we pray, Amen!

Today's Scripture:

I know whom I have believed and am persuaded that he is able to keep that which I have committed unto him against that day (2 Timothy 1:12, KJV).

Associated Scriptures

For God so loved the world that he gave his one and only Son, that whoever believes in him shall not perish but have eternal life (John 3:15).

He who dwells in the shelter of the Most-High will rest in the shadow of the Almighty. I will say of the Lord, "He is my refuge and my fortress, my God, in whom I trust (Psalms 91:1-2).

I lie down and sleep; I wake again, because the Lord sustains me Psalms 3:2.

Correlative Quotes

Love is always itself, and it is love which is exercised and displayed. It is that which fills the mind: everything else is but a means of awakening the soul that dwells in love to its exercise. This is the divine character. No doubt the time of judgment will come; but our relationships with God are in grace. Love is His nature.

It is now the time of its exercise. We represent Him on earth in testimony.[146] – John Nelson Darby

What wonder if men find everything uncertain, when they refuse to bow their intellects to the declarations of the God of truth? Note then with admiration, the refreshing, and even startling positiveness of the apostle—"I know," says he. And that is not enough—"I am persuaded." He speaks like one who cannot tolerate a doubt. There is no question about whether he has believed or not. "I know whom I have believed." There is no question as to whether he was right in so believing. "I am persuaded that he is able to keep that which I have committed to him." There is no suspicion as to the future, for he is as positive for years to come as he is for this present moment. "He is able to keep that which I have committed to him until that day.[147] – Charles Spurgeon

That is, the soul, with all its immortal interests. A man has nothing of higher value to entrust to another than the interests of his soul, and there is no other act of confidence like that in which he entrusts the keeping of that soul to the Son of God.[148] – Albert Barnes

Author's Notes

1. God's Love Saves Us: Ephesians 2:1-5, "*As for you, you were dead in your transgressions and sins, in which you used to live when you followed the ways of this world and of the ruler of the kingdom of the air, the spirit who is now at work in those who are disobedient. All of us also lived among them at one time, gratifying the cravings of our sinful nature and following its desires and thoughts. Like the rest, we were by nature objects of*

---

[146] John Nelson Darby, Synopsis of the Books of the Bible, Public Domain, 1857- 62, Ibid.

[147] Charles Spurgeon, "*Assured Security in Christ*," Public Domain, 1870, spurgeongems.org/vols16-18/chs908.pdf, P. 1.

[148] Albert Barnes, Notes Explanatory and Practical, Public Domain, 1829, Ibid, P. 3959.

wrath. But because of his great love for us, God, who is rich in mercy, made us alive with Christ even when we were dead in transgressions. It is by grace you have been saved.

Paul explains to the church that we were at one time all unrighteous, born in disobedience (Psalm 51:5). That we used to desire the things of the world rather than the blessings of God (Romans 12:2). We lived among those who defied God openly or in secret. Just like others who were ill-behaved, we became the object of God's wrath as we suffered the consequences of sin (Romans 1:18). We shared their desired and participated in the fruits of their delights (Romans 1:21-22). But because of God great love for us, He drew us to Himself (John 12:32). Those who did not refuse the calling of God became His children by grace through the miraculous gift of faith (John 1:12).

2. God's Love Secures Us: Romans 8:38-39, *"For I am convinced that neither death nor life, neither angels nor demons, neither the present nor the future, nor any powers, neither height nor depth, nor anything else in all creation, will be able to separate us from the love of God that is in Christ Jesus our Lord."*

We who *"have tasted the Lord's graciousness"* and as a result have been *"kept by the power of God through faith unto salvation"* (1 Peter 1:5), and grasped and cradled by the arms of humanly unattainable Love? We who are unworthy of God's love have been built up *"in your most holy faith, praying in the Holy Spirit."* Therefore, we must *"keep ourselves in the love of God, waiting expectantly for the mercy of our Lord Jesus Christ for eternal life."* (Jude 20-21, CSB).

Nothing has the power to separate us from the love of God; nothing. Our position in Christ is secure. Nothing but God has the power to change our hearts. That which His Spirit secures cannot be separated.

Not only is there nothing in this world that can cause this separation, but we also cannot separate ourselves from God. There is no action of mankind that can sever the salvation of those who have received the Holy Spirit. Romans 8:39 uses the phrase "nor anything else in all creation" (NIV, ESV, AMP) or "nor any other created thing" (NKJV, NASB, HCSB). All six of these translations say the same thing, nothing that is created can separate us from God's love. Since we are a created thing (Psalm 139:13), we cannot break our own relationship with God. Just as we can do nothing to receive eternal life, we can do nothing to cause it to be taken away; nothing.

3. The Love of God Shelters Us: Psalms 61:4, "*I long to dwell in your tent forever and take refuge in the shelter of your wings.*"

How wonderful our God. He provides a place of comfort for us (Psalm 23:1). God's Spirit guides us when we pay attention to His directions (Psalm 23:3). Even when we find ourselves in untenable situations far too difficult for us to control, God provides comfort as He walks with us through the troubling situations of life (Psalm 23:4). Jesus provides for our every need even when the situations look hopeless and the creditors of this world surround us, He is there with His mercy and blessings (Psalm 23:5). Christ's close attention to our lives surrounds and shields us now and until He comes again in glory (Psalm 23:6).

"For in the day of trouble he will keep me safe in his dwelling; he will hide me in the shelter of his sacred tent and set me high upon a rock" (Psalm 27:5).

4. The Love of God Sustains Us: Psalms 54:4, "*Surely God is my help, the Lord is the one who sustains me.*"

God sustains us in this life through faith and hope. Faith is the gift of God which is given to us by an act of grace. Hope sustains us (Romans 5:2). Hope is given to us as a reassurance of our salvation and position with God (Ephesians 1:13-14). Hope is an expression of the promises of God. As we read and study His word, the Bible, we begin to see the myriad of promises and expressions of love in its pages (Galatians 5:5).

Spiritual Application

Because it contains in itself the root of the other two: we believe only one whom we love, we hope only that which we love. And thus, the forms of Faith and Hope which will there forever subsist, will be sustained in, and overshadowed by, the all-pervading superior element of eternal Love.[149] – Henry Alford

In The Book Of 1 Corinthians, Paul Is addressing The Many infractions of this misdirected Church. Chapter 13 is a welcome but planned break in the middle of accusations about the misconduct that was rampant in the church at Corinth. This was a disobedient church!

1 Corinthians chapter 13 contains several important truths. In section one, verses 1-3 is considered to be the introduction to this chapter and has three principle thoughts. In essence verse 1 says that when we speak without love we say nothing. Secondly, when we have all knowledge, understanding, and teach all the mysteries of scripture yet without love we are nothing. Finally, if we can make the greatest human sacrifices for others but they are accomplished outside of love, we gain nothing.

Section 2, verses 4-7 begins with the statement, "Love is patient, love is kind. This truth precedes and introduces a long list of what love is not. This entire list can be avoided through our use of patience and kindness which lead to the actions listed in verse 7.

In section 3, we see that *"Love never fails"* (vs. 8). Every other work of the church pails when we consider the importance of love.

In section 4. Paul closes the chapter with this interesting statement: *Now these three remain: faith, hope, and love...but the greatest of these is love* (vs. 13). Love never fails since it is eternal. We will no longer need faith and hope when we see Jesus (1 Thessalonians 4:13-18). Our faith and hope will both be fulfilled.

When believing is impossible, when even hoping seems utterly out of the question, love endures. It does not get angry, it does not give up, it loves on, works on, endures on. Let Jesus serve as an illustration. How long Jesus has borne with men, but for love He has gotten back

[149] Henry Alford, The New Testament for English Readers, Volume 2, The Epistles of Paul, Public Domain, Gilbert and Rivington Printers, St. John's Square, London, 1872, P. 221.

only reproach and sneers and spitting and blows and crucifixion. Reproach has broken His heart, and He is fast dying, but He summons all His waning strength, and cries, "Father forgive them, for they know not what they do" (Luk_23:24). That was love.[150] – R. A. Torrey

Lessons within the Lesson

How is God's grace related to God's love? Read 1 Timothy 1:14.

Explain how we can know that we have eternal security in Jesus. Read Romans 8:38-39.

How does the love of God sustain us in both good times and bad? Read Psalm 18:35.

Why is love considered the greatest gift from God?

---

[150] R. A. Torrey, *Love Contrasted, Described, Exalted (1 Corinthians 13)* R. A. Torrey Collection, Public Domain, bible.prayerrequest.com/1297-ra-torrey-collection-80-files/38/154/.

31. EPILOGUE – LOVE: THE FINAL THOUGHTS

Prayer

Who can discern his errors? Forgive my hidden faults. Keep your servant also from willful sins; may they not rule over me. Then will I be blameless, innocent of great transgression. May the words of my mouth and the meditation of my heart be pleasing in your sight, O Lord, my Rock and my Redeemer (Psalms 19:12-14).

Author's Notes

OUR LIVES EXPRESSED IN OUR WORDS, WORKS, AND WALK

Though I speak with the tongues of men and of angels, but have not love, I have become sounding brass or a clanging cymbal. And though I have the gift of prophecy, and understand all mysteries and all knowledge, and though I have all faith, so that I could remove mountains, but have not love, I am nothing. And though I bestow all my goods to feed the poor, and though I give my body to be burned, but have not love, it profits me nothing (1 Corinthians 13:1-3).

Although I can speak with otherworldly eloquence, but my heart is void of God's love, I say nothing! In life in general, we should not dominate the talking, but instead, dominate the listening. The old saying, "That's why God gave us two ears and one mouth" has never been more appropriate than in today's world. When we do speak, our words should be uplifting and motivating. We should speak words that encourage not disparage others.

Our God is a God of inspiration. He explains Himself in Isaiah 41:10 (NLT), *"Don't be afraid, for I am with you. Don't be discouraged, for I am your God. I will strengthen you and help you. I will hold you up with my victorious right hand."* Jesus states in John

16:33 (NLT), *"I have told you all this so that you may have peace in me. Here on earth, you will have many trials and sorrows. But take heart, because I have overcome the world."* Therefore, our words should empathize not correct and scold. Our words should edify and be a living language that encourages closeness to God.

Though I am the best preacher, teacher, or communicator of God's word. Though I seem learned, eloquent, wise, and relevant in my interpretation and presentation. Though I have faith that seems undaunted by the temptations of this world and have not love, I am nothing! Our attitude must proclaim the glory of God (Psalm 19:14).

Our understanding should reflect the nature of God. Our faith must challenge others to greater faith. Our lives must be used to magnify Christ It should not be viewed as an opportunity to vault ourselves.

Finally, though I seemingly give all that I have to help others. Though I sacrifice my own body on the crosses of this life and don't show the love of God in the process. If I do all things without reflecting His love, all of my works will be meaningless and empty, gaining nothing in the end.

My motive is critical. The works that we accomplish in this life, even though they may be "good works" in the eyes of the world, mean nothing if we have the wrong motive. What we have in our hearts means everything. 1 Samuel 16:7 (NLT) substantiates this truth when it says, *"The LORD doesn't see things the way you see them. People judge by outward appearance, but the LORD looks at the heart."*

A LIFE THAT REFLECTS JESUS

The traces of imperfection which we see in Job prove all the more powerfully that divine grace can make grand examples out of common constitutions and that keen feelings of indignation under injustice need not prevent a man's becoming a model of patience. I am thankful that I know that Job did speak somewhat bitterly and proved himself a man, for now I know that it was a man like myself who said, "The Lord gave, and the Lord has taken away; blessed be the name of the Lord." It was a man of flesh and blood such as mine, who said, "Shall we receive good at the hands of God, and shall we not receive evil?" Yes, it was a man of like passions with myself who said, "Though He slay me, yet will I trust in Him.[151] – Charles Spurgeon

A life that reflects Jesus is characterized by patience and kindness. We have all been impatient and suffered the consequences. Impatience causes stress. Stress finds its end in either frustration or fear. Neither of these two results honors or glorifies God.

Patience cannot be learned. It is a gift from God. The answer to impatience is Godly composure. Proverbs 3:5-6 instructs us to, "*Trust in the LORD with all your heart and lean not on your own understanding; in all your ways submit to him, and he will make your paths straight.*"

Impatience is the enemy of objective, rational thought and the birthplace of stress and anxiety. Anxiety leads to fear and uncertainty. Reality is seldom worse than perception. We must focus on patience and wait for the reality before we react. God is in charge of all things. God's promise is that all things will work together for our good (Romans 8:28).

There are several steps that we can take to relieve stress. The first involves submission. We must understand God's will for our lives and place our full trust in Him. Proverbs 3:5-6 tells us to "*Trust in the Lord with all our heats and lean not on our own understanding. In all your ways submit to him, and he will make your paths straight.*" The second step requires continued spiritual growth. Ephesians 4:15 (ESV) requires that we, "*...speak the truth in love and grow up in all aspects into Him who is the head, even Christ...*" Next, we are obligated to repent continually for our disobedient actions. To repent means to turn around and go in the other direction. Acts 3:19 explains, "*Therefore repent and turn back,*

---

[151] Charles Spurgeon, The Pearl of Patience, Public Domain, 1911, spurgeongems.org/vols55-57, chs355.pdf, P. 2.

so that your sins may be wiped out..." Finally, pray for God to give you the gift of patience. Philippians 4:6, "*Do not be anxious about anything, but in every situation, by prayer and petition, with thanksgiving, present your requests to God.*"

In addition to patience, God's love requires kindness. We must be kind to one another in all circumstances. Mature, loving Christians take the lead when it comes to kindness. Kindness, along with patience, are two of the fruits of the Spirit (Galatians 5:22). The believer must clothe themselves in kindness (Colossians 3:12)

Finally, we see in 1 Corinthians 13:8 that "*love never fails.*" It never fails because it is the greatest of all of the gifts we receive as a believer in Christ. Both grace and faith come from love. Love represents the foundation upon which our relationship with God is established and maintained. God's love is unconditional. Therefore, He loves those who have been called His children with a deep, abiding, and everlasting love.

Love never fails because nothing can or will ever separate us from the love of God (Romans 8:38). A love that was born out of creation and sealed through the death, burial, and resurrection of Jesus, His Son. All praise, honor, and glory to Him who sits on the throne for eternity (Revelation 5:13).

BIBLIOGRAPHY

Albert Barnes, Notes Explanatory and Practical, Public Domain, Blackie and Son, Queen Street, Glasgow, South College Street, Edinburgh, and Warwick Square, London, 1845, Free Download, Archive.org.

Henry Alford, The New Testament for English Readers, Volume 2, The Epistles of Paul, Public Domain, Gilbert and Rivington Printers, St. John's Square, London, 1872.

Andrews University Seminary Studies, Spring 1989, Vol. 27, No. 1, 1-19. Copyright © 1989 by Andrews University Press.Frank Binford Hole, Hole's Old and New Testament Commentary, Public Domain, stempublishing.com/authors/hole/.

Fr. Fred Bobosh, On Pentecost, What Language was Heard, orthochristian.com/ 104031.html., Blog -06/05/2017.

John Calvin, Commentaries on the Catholic Epistles, Rights: Public Domain, URL: ccel.org/ccel/calvin/calcom 45.html., Publisher: Grand Rapids, MI.

John Calvin, Commentary on Isaiah, Quote is Public Domain, rtc.edu.au/RTC/media/ Documents/Vox%20articles/Prophecy-in-the-Reformed-Tradition-BB-60-1995.

Adam Clarke, The Adam Clarke Commentary Corinthians through Philemon, Public Domain, © 1836, Thomas Tegg and Son, 73 Cheapside, London. godrules.net/library/clarke/clarkegen 1.htm.

Adam Clarke, The Adam Clarke Commentary, John to Romans, Public Domain, 1836, Thomas Tegg and Son, 73 Cheapside, London. godrules.net/library/clarke/clarkegen 1.htm.

Adam Clarke, The New Testament of our Lord and Savior Jesus Christ, A Commentary and Critical Notes, Romans to Revelation, T. Mason and G. Lane Publishers, New York.

Thomas Constable, Expository Notes of Dr. Thomas Constable, Public Domain, planobiblechapel.org/constable-notes/.

John Nelson Darby, Synopsis of the Books of the Bible, Public Domain, 1857- 62, stempublishing.com/authors/darby/synopsis/.

Matthew George Easton, Illustrated Bible Dictionary, Third Edition, published by Thomas Nelson, 1897, Public Domain, ntslibrary.com/PDF%20Books/Eastons%20Bible%20 Dictionary.pdf, (copy freely).

Jonathan Edwards, Undetected Spiritual Pride – One Cause of Failure in Times of Revival, grace-abounding.com/Articles/Sin/Pride_Edwards.htm.

C. J. Ellicott, (Charles John), A New Testament Commentary for English Readers, 1819-1905. Public Domain, Published by E. D. Dolton and Company, New York, 1897.

Joseph S. Excell, The Bible Illustrator, Vol. 27, 1 Corinthians Vol. 1, Public Domain, 1849, Anson D. F. Randolph and Company, New York, New York.

John Gill, John Gill's Exposition of the Entire Bible, 1810, Public Domain, Mathews & Leigh, London.

Robert Hawker, The Poor Man's New Testament Commentary, Volume 2, 1805, Public Domain, Printed by W. Nicholson, Warner Street, London.

Matthew Henry, Matthew Henry Commentary on the Whole Bible (Unabridged), Volume III (Job to Song of Solomon), Public Domain, 1706, bitimage.dyndns. org/.

Matthew Henry, Matthew Henry Concise Commentary on the Whole Bible (Unabridged), Volume V (Job to Song of Solomon), Public Domain, 1706, bitimage.dyndns. org/.

Matthew Henry, Matthew Henry Concise Commentary on the Whole Bible (Unabridged), Volume VI, Acts to Revelation, Public Domain, 1706, bitimage.dyndns. org/.

Jamieson, Robert, D. D.; Fausset, A. R.; Brown, David, Commentary Critical and Explanatory on the Whole Bible, Public Domain 1871, Public Domain, Copy Freely.A. T. Robertson, New Testament Word Pictures Volume 6, this work is in the Public Domain. Copy Freely, hopefaithprayer.com/books/NewTestamentWork Pictures-Robertson.pdf.

Martin Luther, Faith is a busy, living, active, mighty thing, tollelege.wordpress.com/2011/02/11/faith-is-a-living-busy-active-mighty-thing-by-martin-luther/, Public Domain.

Fredrick Brotherton Meyer, Our Daily Homily, Public Domain, Grand Rapids, 1899, MI: Christian Fleming H. Revell Company, enduringword.com/downloads/our-daily-homily/.

Edward Mote, My Hope is Built on Nothing Less, 1863, Public Domain, digitalhymnal.org.htlm.

A. T. Robertson, New Testament Word Pictures Volume 6, this work is in the Public Domain. Copy Freely, hopefaithprayer.com/books/NewTestamentWord Pictures-Robertson.pdf.

H. D. M. Spence and Joseph S. Exell, The Pulpit Commentary, Public Domain, Funk & Wagnalls Company New York And Toronto.

Charles Spurgeon, A Song of My Beloved no. 3185 a sermon published on Thursday, February 17, 1910, Metropolitan Tabernacle, Newington. spurgeongems.org/vols55-57/chs3185.pdf.

Charles Spurgeon, "Assured Security in Christ," Public Domain, 1870, spurgeongems.org/vols16-18/chs908.pdf.

Charles Spurgeon, Cure for Envy, Public Domain, charlesspurgeon.nl/jaloezie-2/?lang=en.

Charles Spurgeon, Eternal Faithfulness Unaffected by Human Belief, Public Domain, spurgeongems.org/vols25-27/chs1453.pdf, P. 5

Charles Spurgeon, Heart-Knowledge of God, 1874, Public Domain, spurgeon.org/resource-library/sermons/heart-knowledge-of-god#flipbook/,

Charles Spurgeon, Immeasurable Love, Public Domain, 1885, .romans45.org/spurgeon/sermons/1850.htm.

Charles Spurgeon, Jesus Angry with Hard Hearts , romans45.org/ spurgeon/ sermons/ 1893.htm.

Charles Spurgeon, Life by Faith, Public Domain, 1868, liveprayer.com/spurgeon-sermons.cfm?s=187478.

Charles Spurgeon, "Non Nobis Domine," Public Domain, 1878, spurgeongems.org/vols46-48/chs2784.pdf.

Charles Spurgeon, Now and Then, Public Domain, Sermon #1002, spurgeongems.org/ vols16-18/chs1002.pdf.

Charles Spurgeon, Oh, How He Loves! Public Domain, No. 3228 Delivered by C. H. Spurgeon, at The Metropolitan Tabernacle, Newington, On Lord's-Day Evening, July 7, 1872.

Charles Spurgeon, Pride and Humility, 1856, Public Domain, spurgeon.org/resource-library/sermons/pride-and-humility#flipbook/.

Charles Spurgeon, Rare Fruit, spurgeongems.org/vols25-27/chs1558.pdf.

Charles Spurgeon, " Saved in Hope, Public Domain, 1881, spurgeongems.org/vols25-27/chs1616.pdf.

Charles Spurgeon, Serving the Lord, Public Domain, 1869, spurgeongems.org/vols13-15/chs885.pdf.

Charles Spurgeon, Spurgeon Quotes, Public Domain, princeofpreachers.org/quotes/ category/love-of-christ. P. 1

Charles Spurgeon, The Pearl of Patience, Public Domain, 1911, spurgeongems.org/ vols55-57, chs355.pdf, P. 2.

Charles Spurgeon, The Universal Remedy, Public Domain, 1868, spurgeongems.org/ vols13-15/chs834.pdf.

Charles Spurgeon, There is Forgiveness, Public Domain, 1877, spurgeongems.org/vols40-42/chs2422.pdf.

Charles Spurgeon, Vanities and Verities, Public Domain, spurgeongems.org/vols22-24/chs1380.pd.

James Strong, Strong's Exhaustive Concordance, © 1890, Public Domain, Copy Freely, Christian Classic Reprints.

R. A. Torrey, Love Contrasted, Described, Exalted (1 Corinthians 13) R. A. Torrey Collection, Public Domain, bible.prayerrequest.com/1297-ra-torrey-collection-80-files/38/154/.

Benjamin B. Warfield, Counterfeit Miracles, Public Domain, 1919, monergism.com/thethreshold/sdg/warfield/warfield_counterfeit.html.

John Wesley, John Wesley's Notes of the Bible, Public Domain, Publication date 1755, jacobjuncker.files.wordpress.com/2010/03/wesley-explanatory-notes-on-the-bible.pdf#page=564&zoom=100,0,308, P. 319.

Andy Williams, Love is a Many Splendored Thing, metrolyrics.com/love-is-a-many-splendored-thing-lyrics-andy-williams.html